COLORING BOOK FOR KIDS

LION

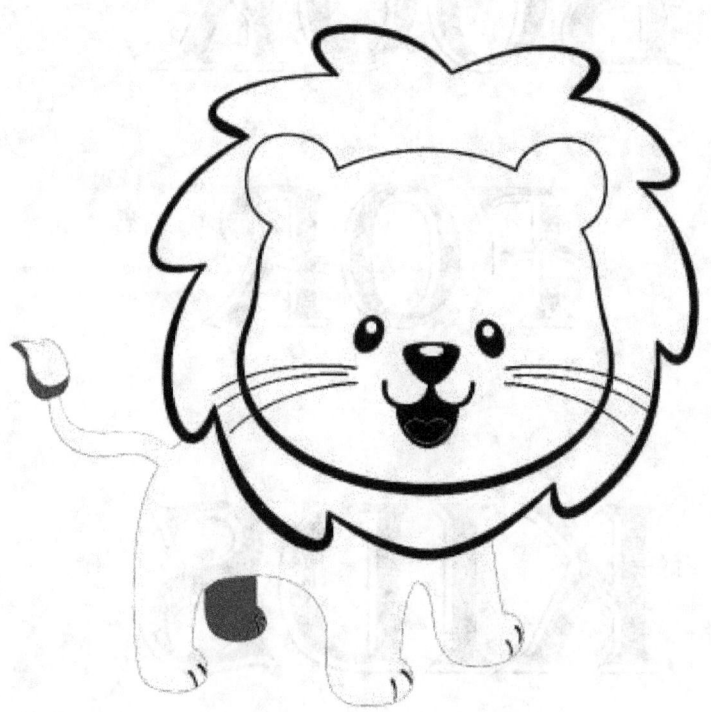

CAT

TIGER

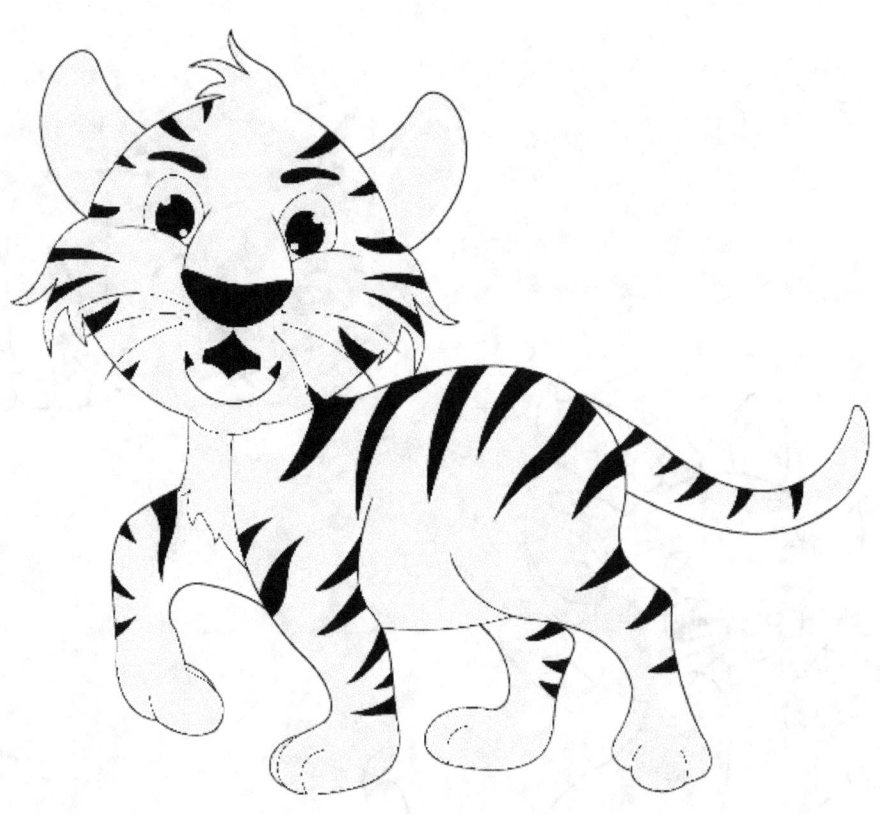

SNAK

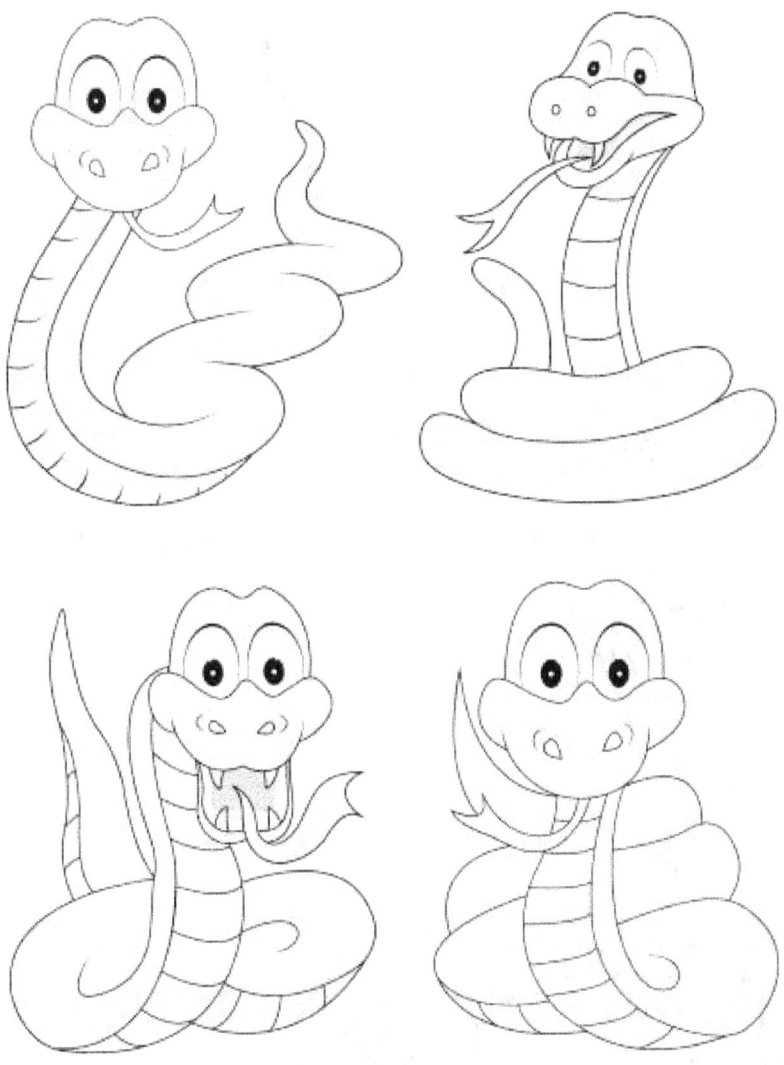

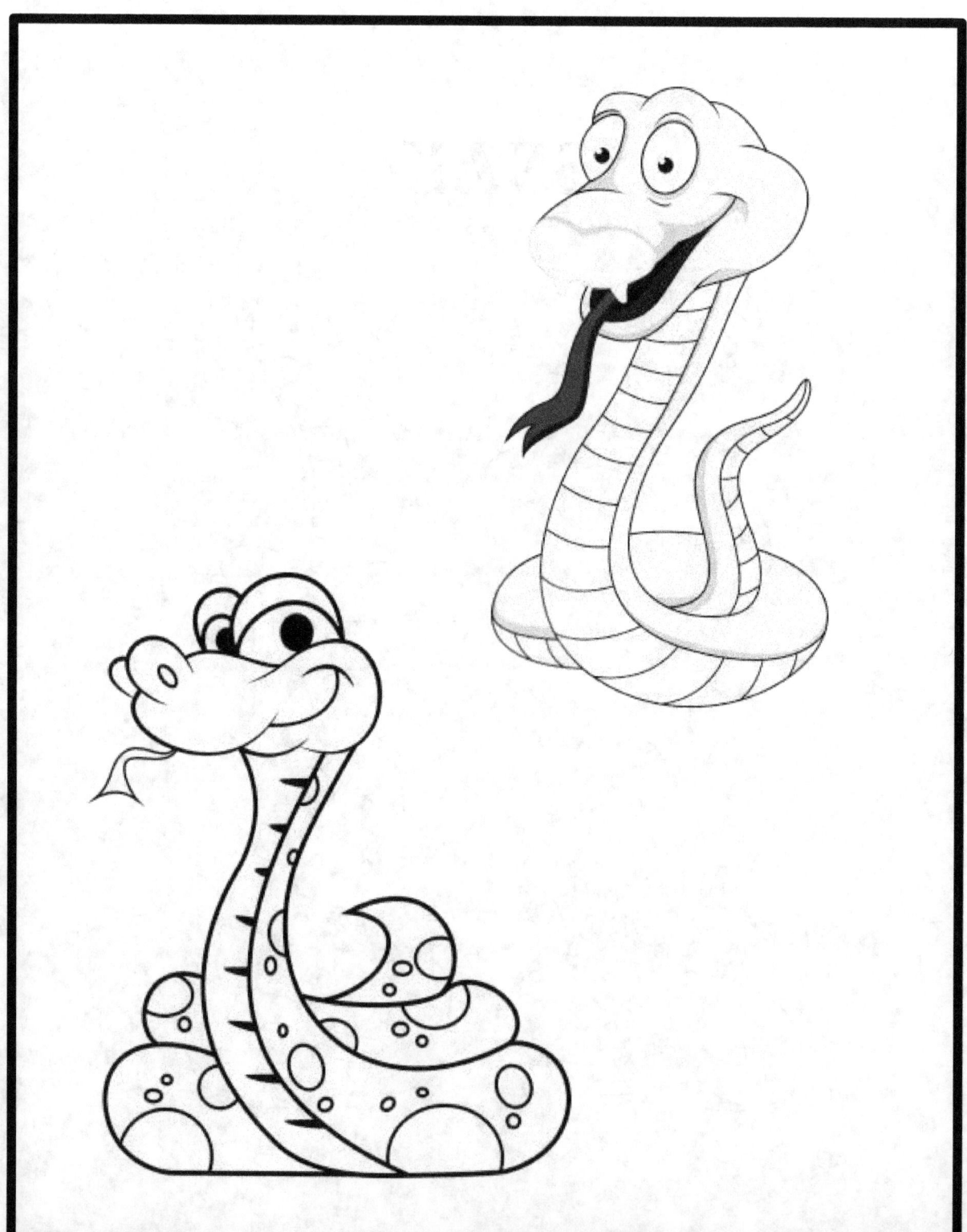

FROG

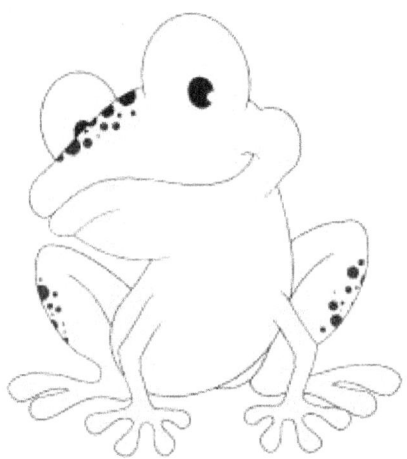
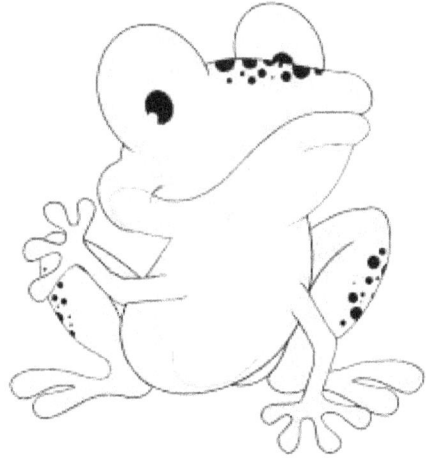
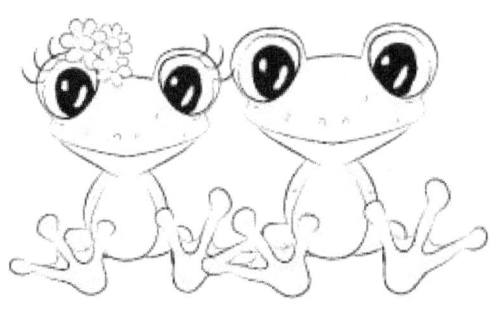
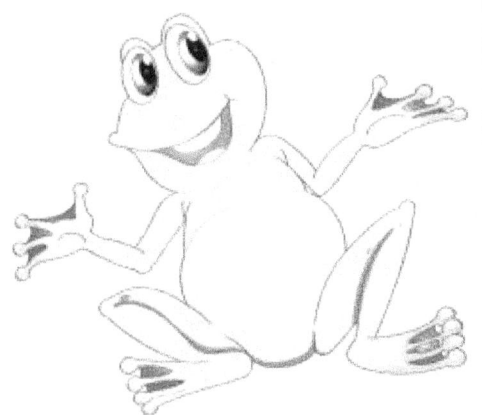

RABBIT

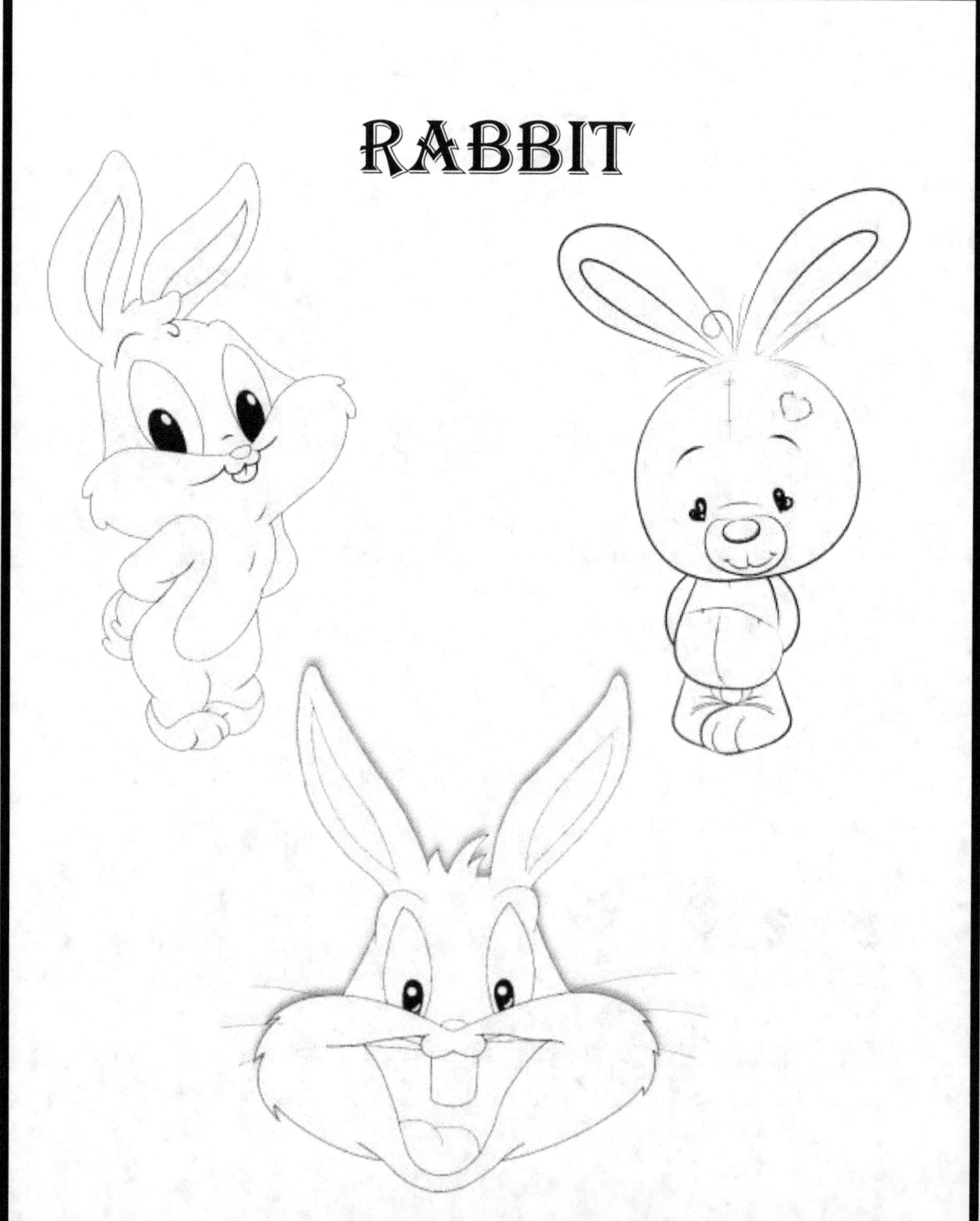

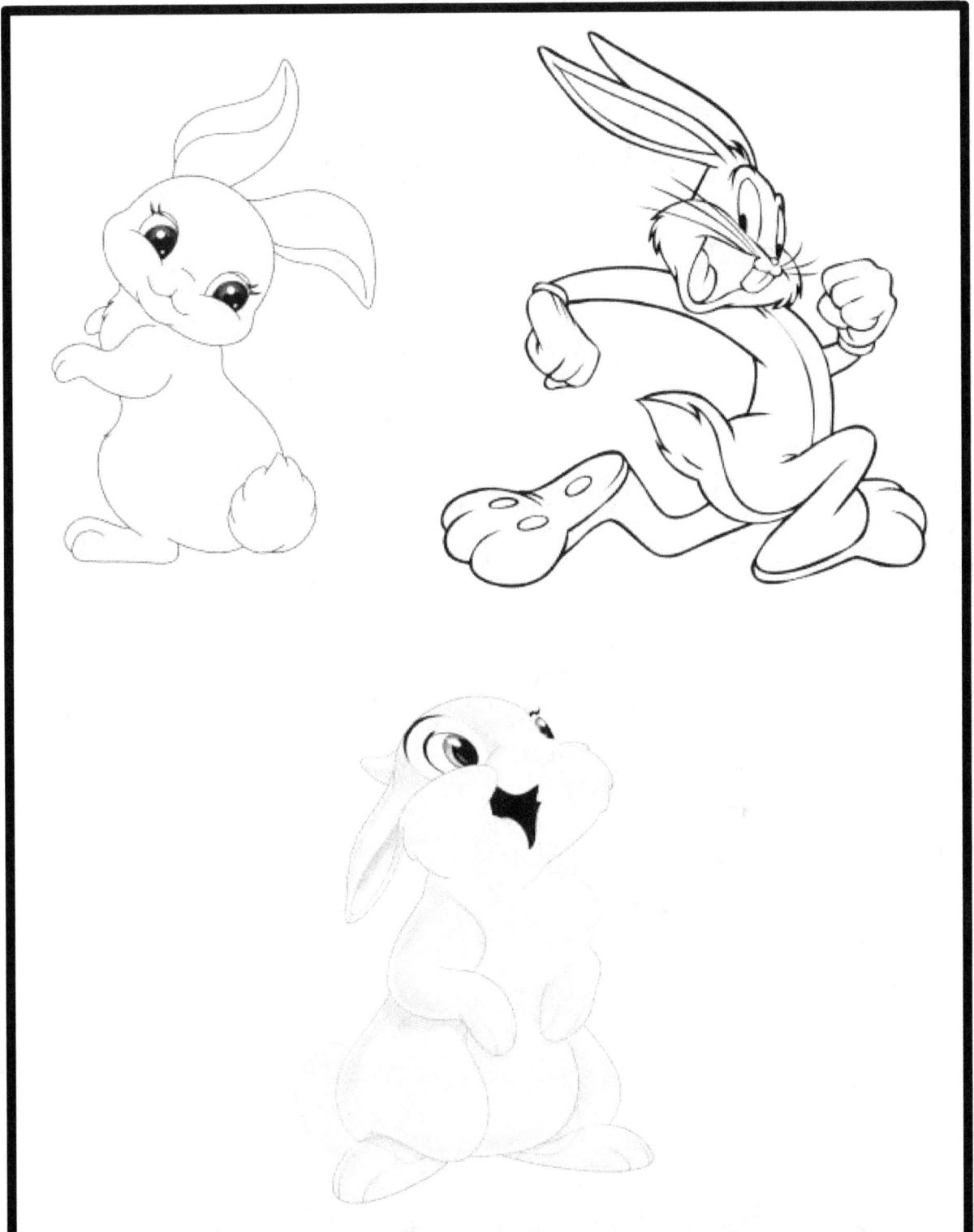

ELEPHANT

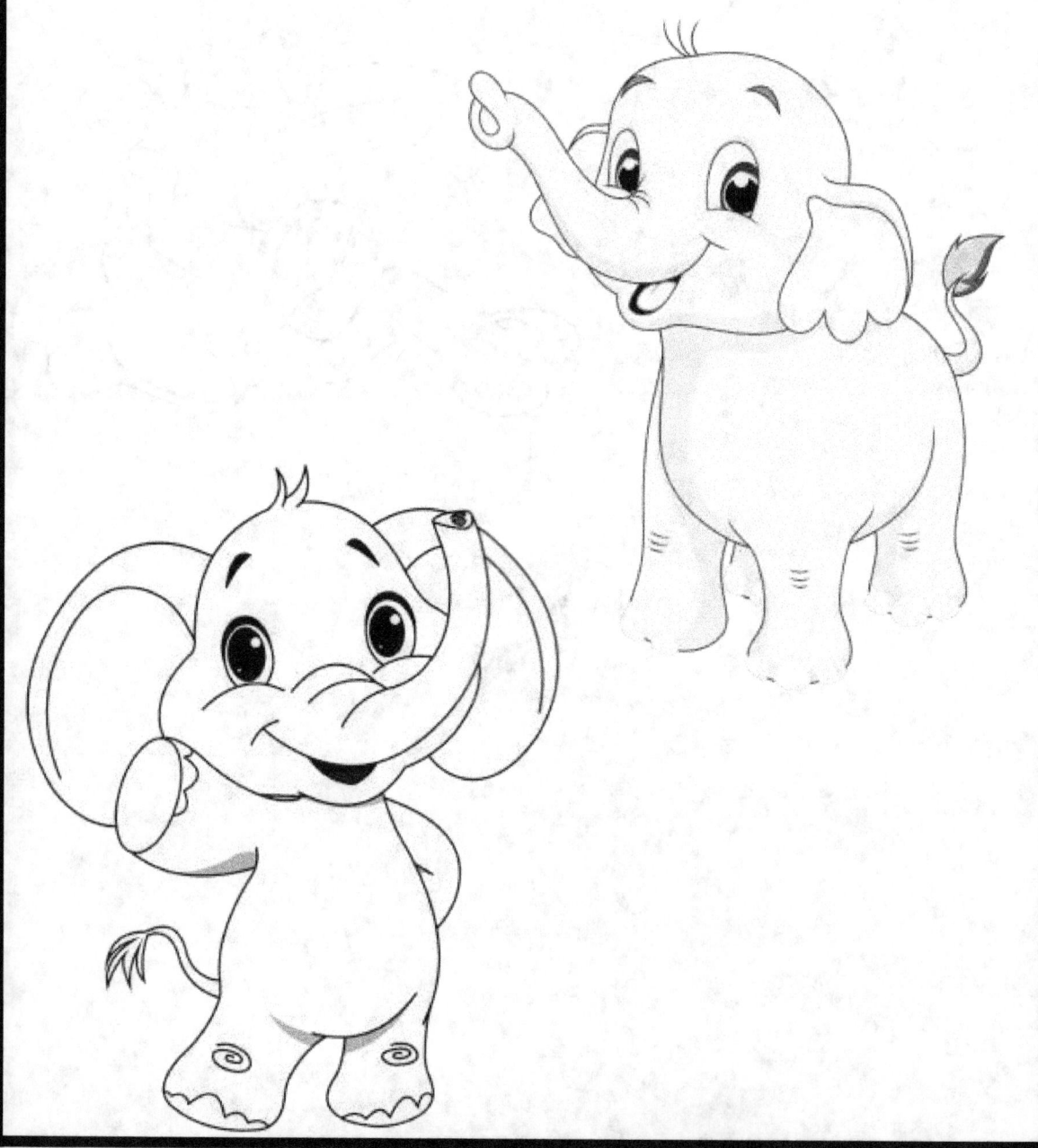

BIRD

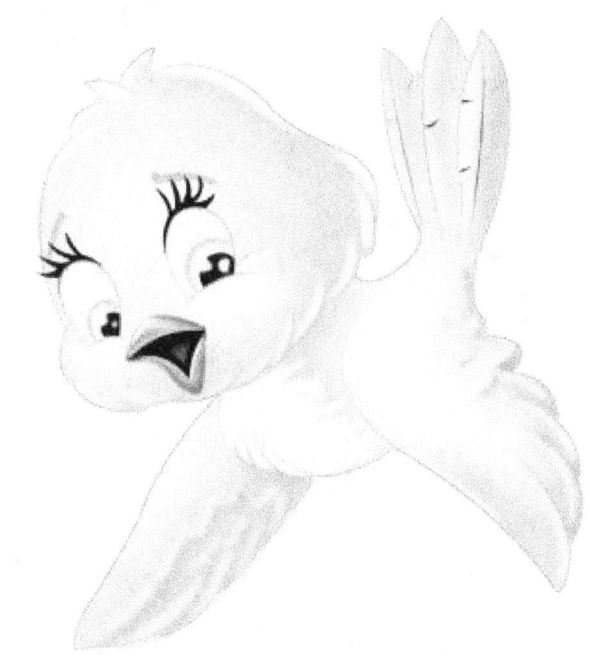

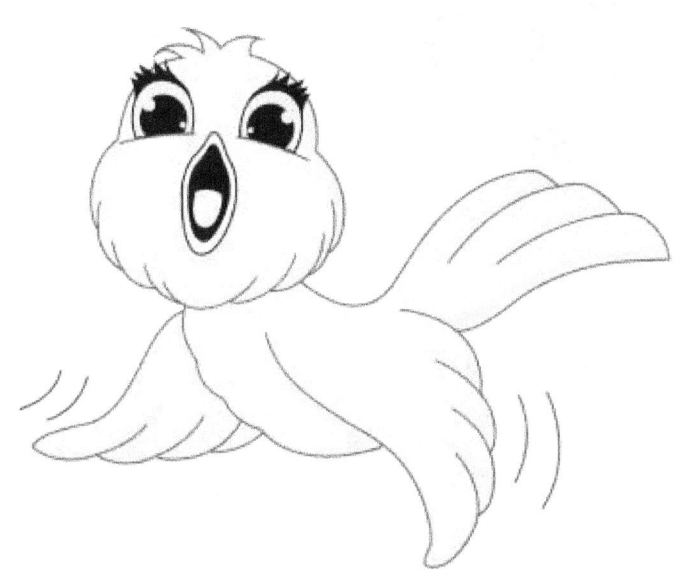

BEE

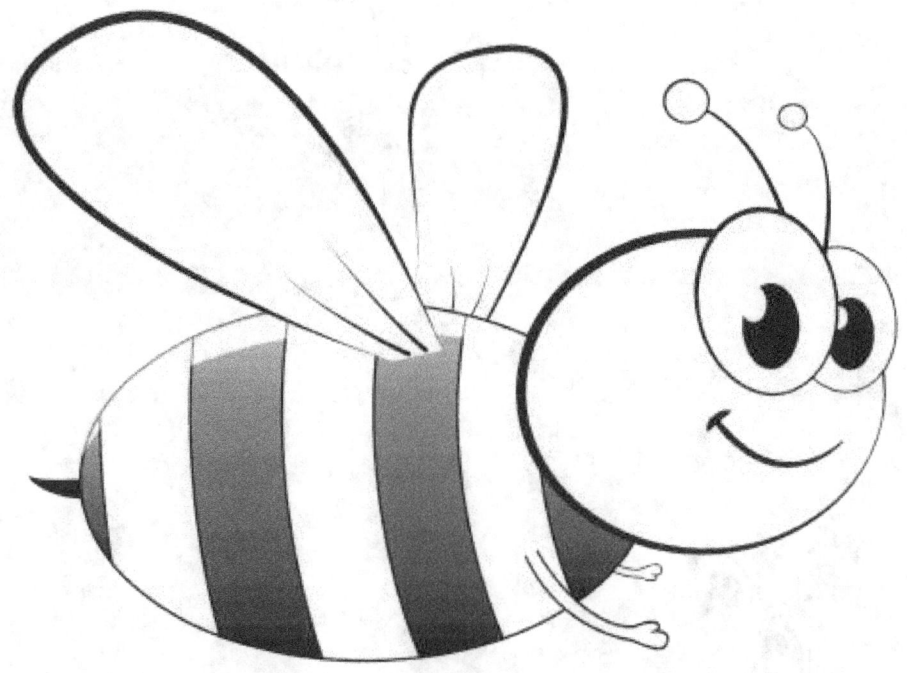

ZEBRA

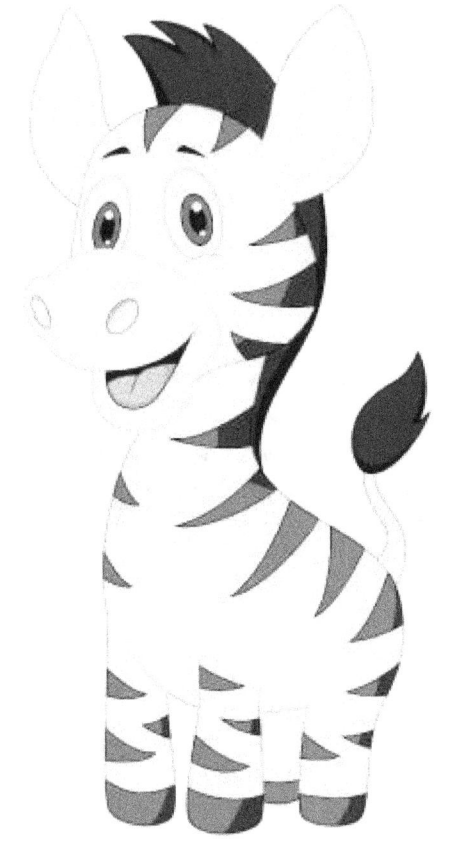
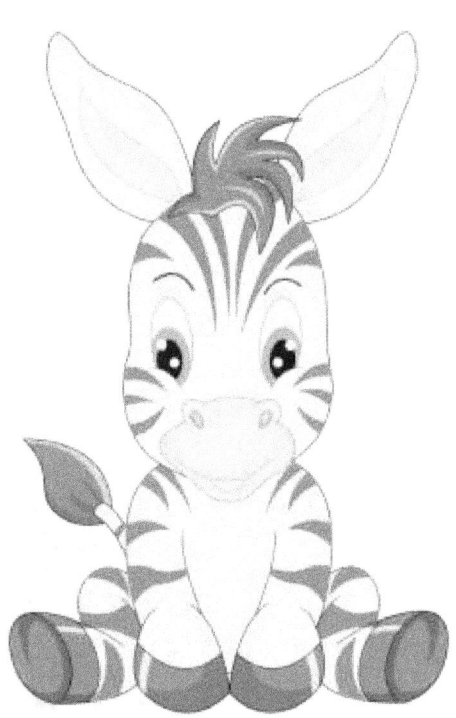

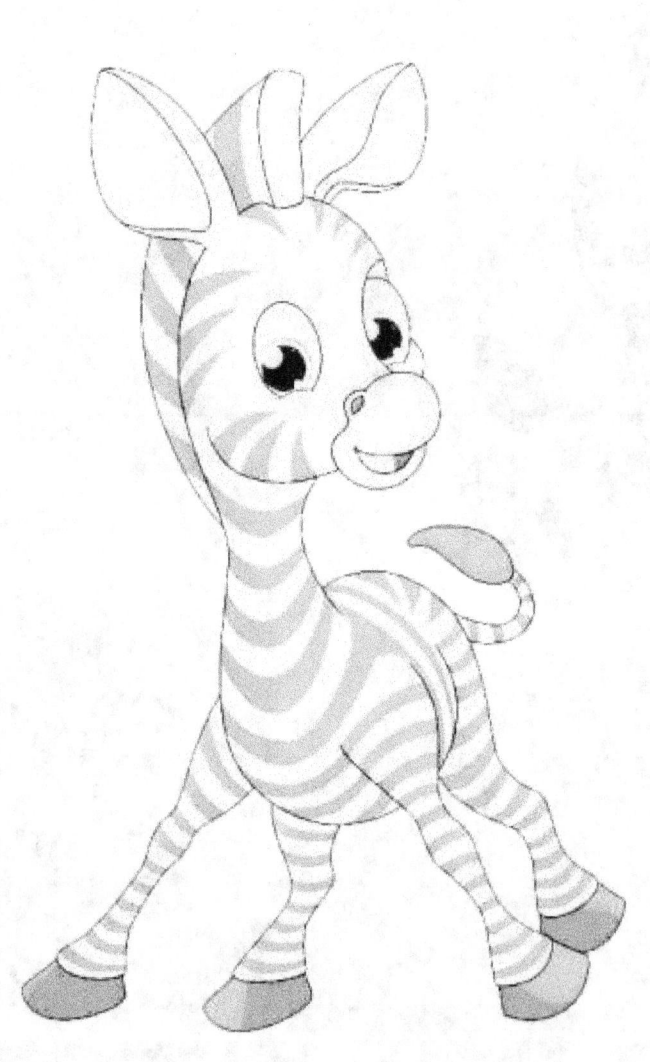

GIRAFFE

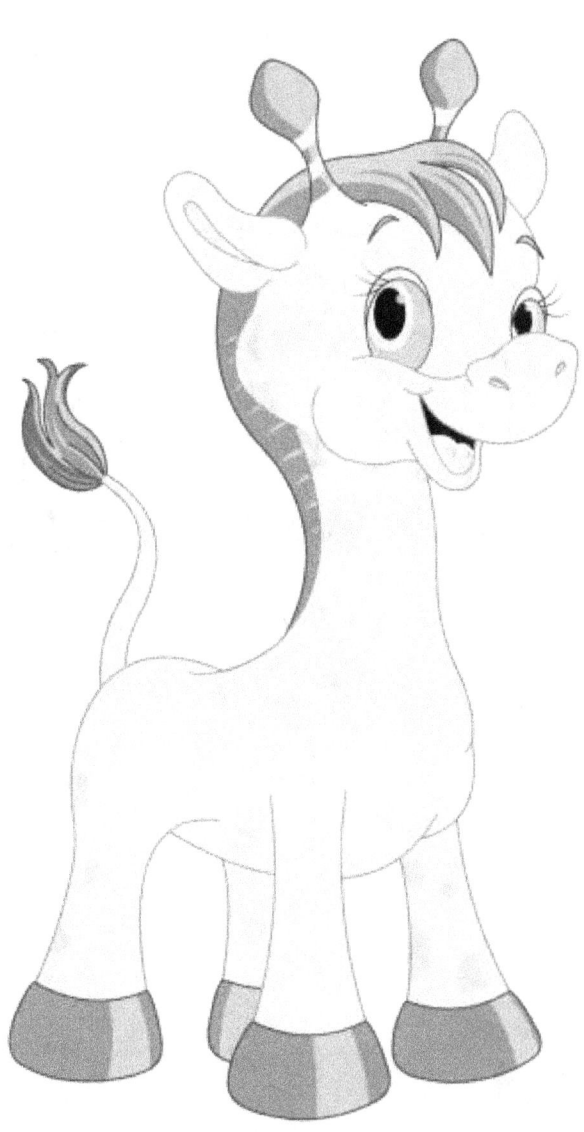

SHEEP

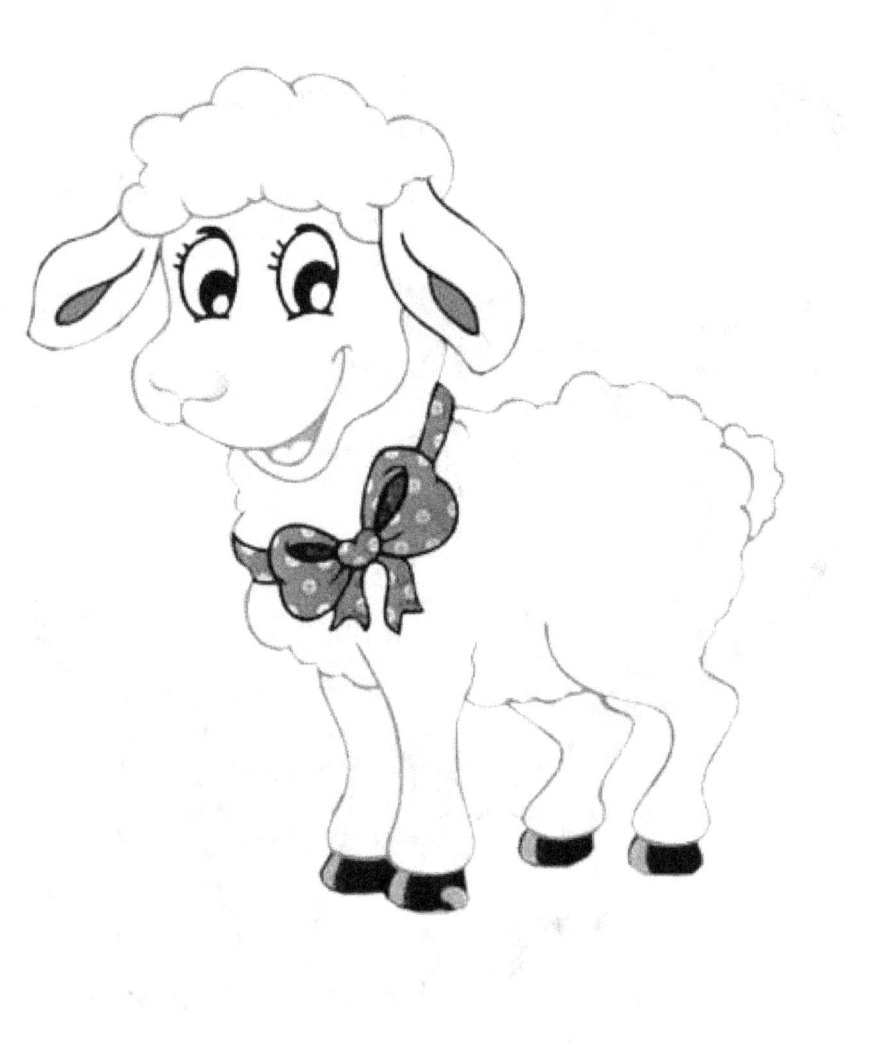

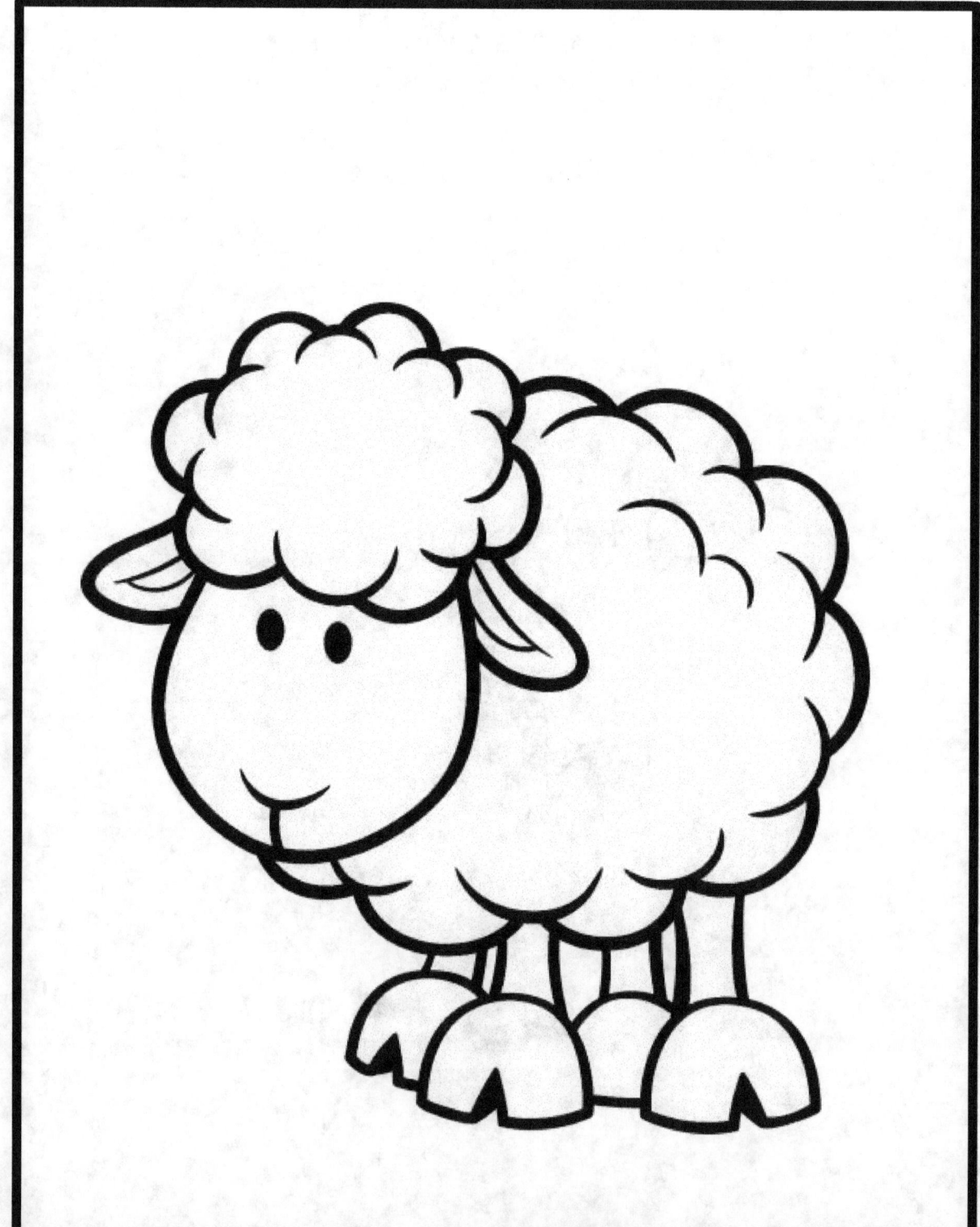

CHIKEN

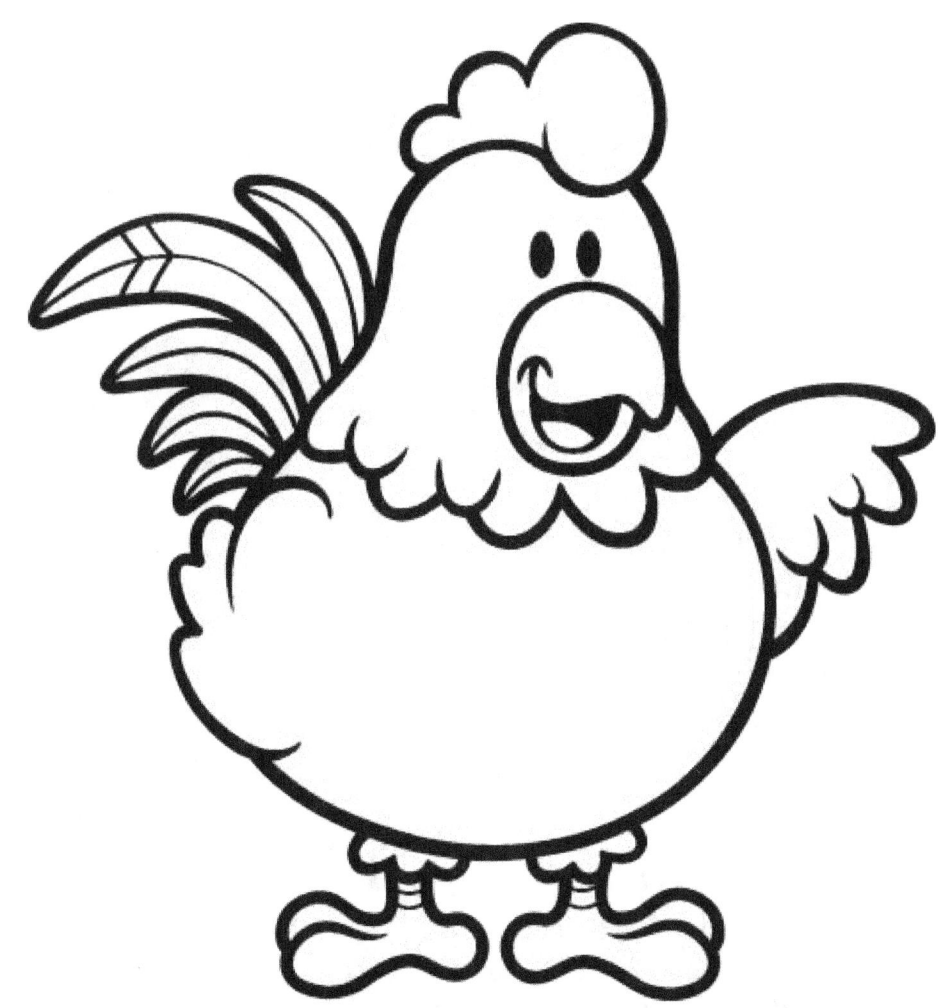

DEER

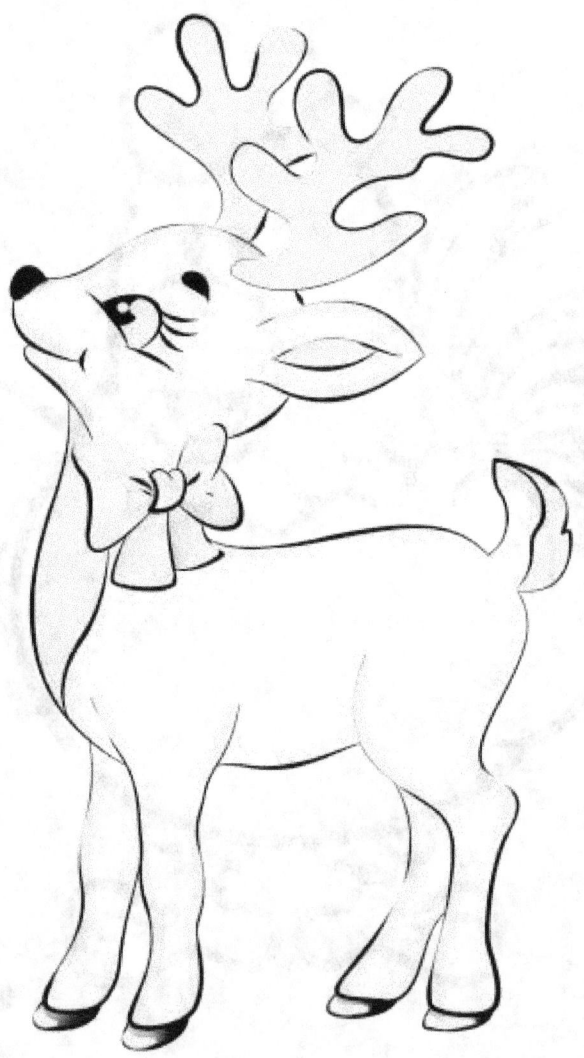

OWL

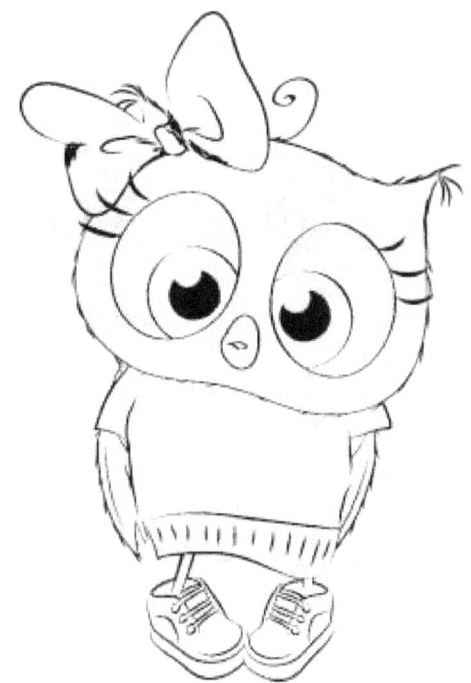

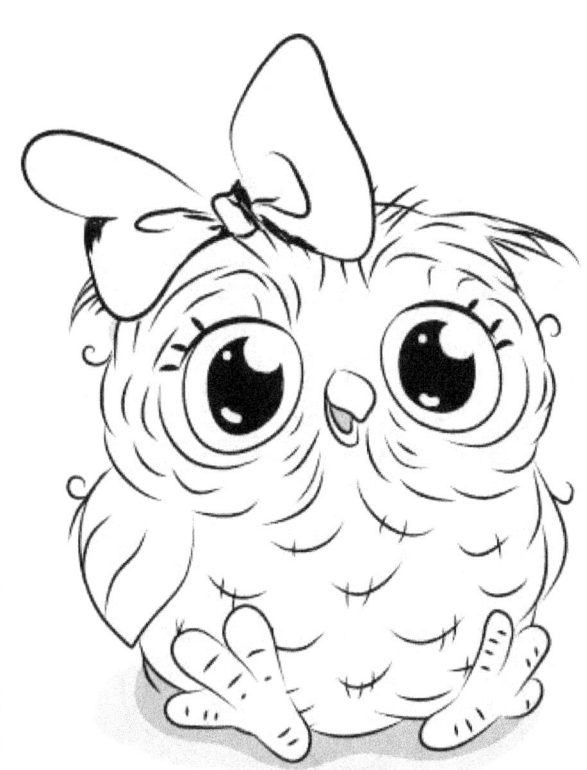

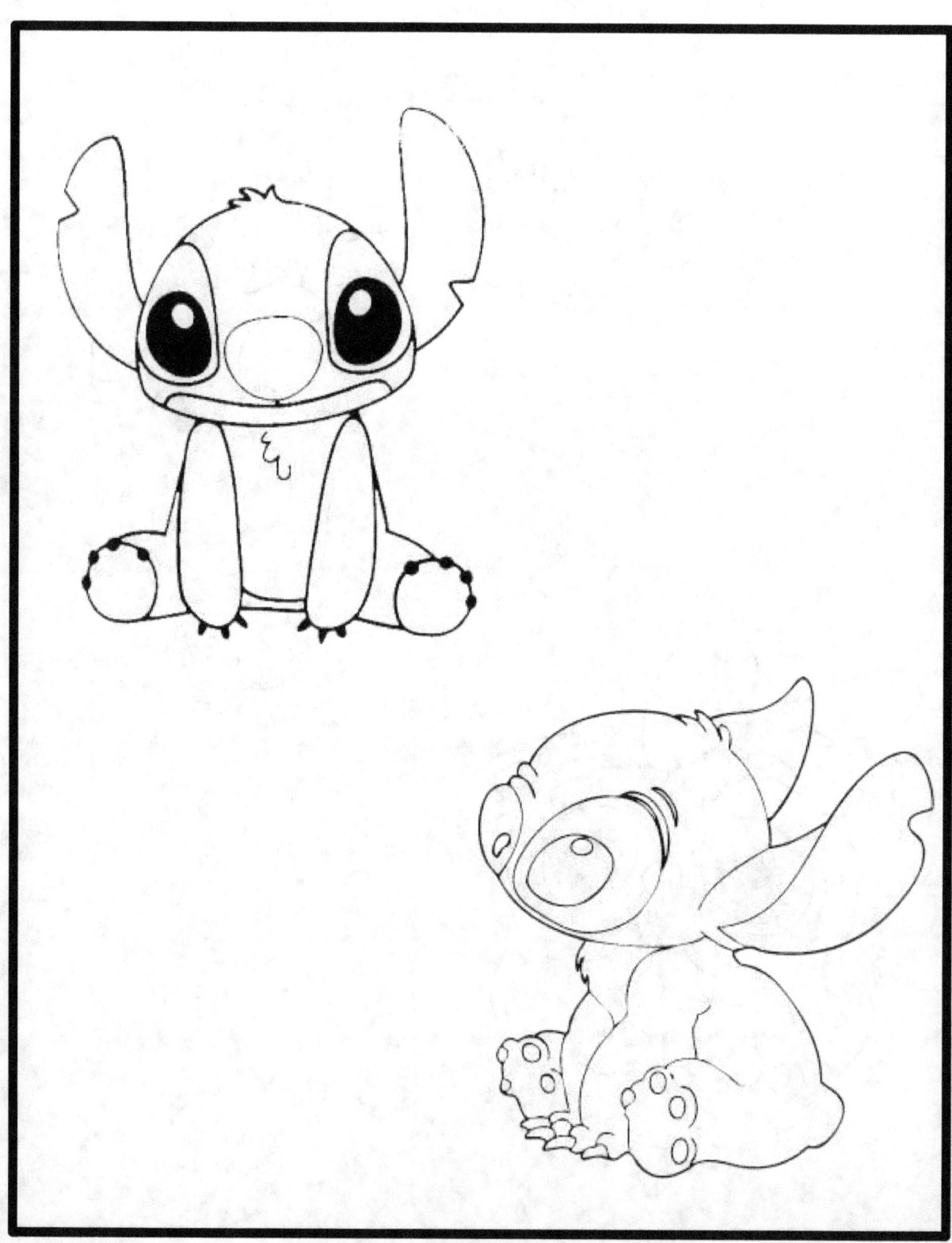

DONKEY

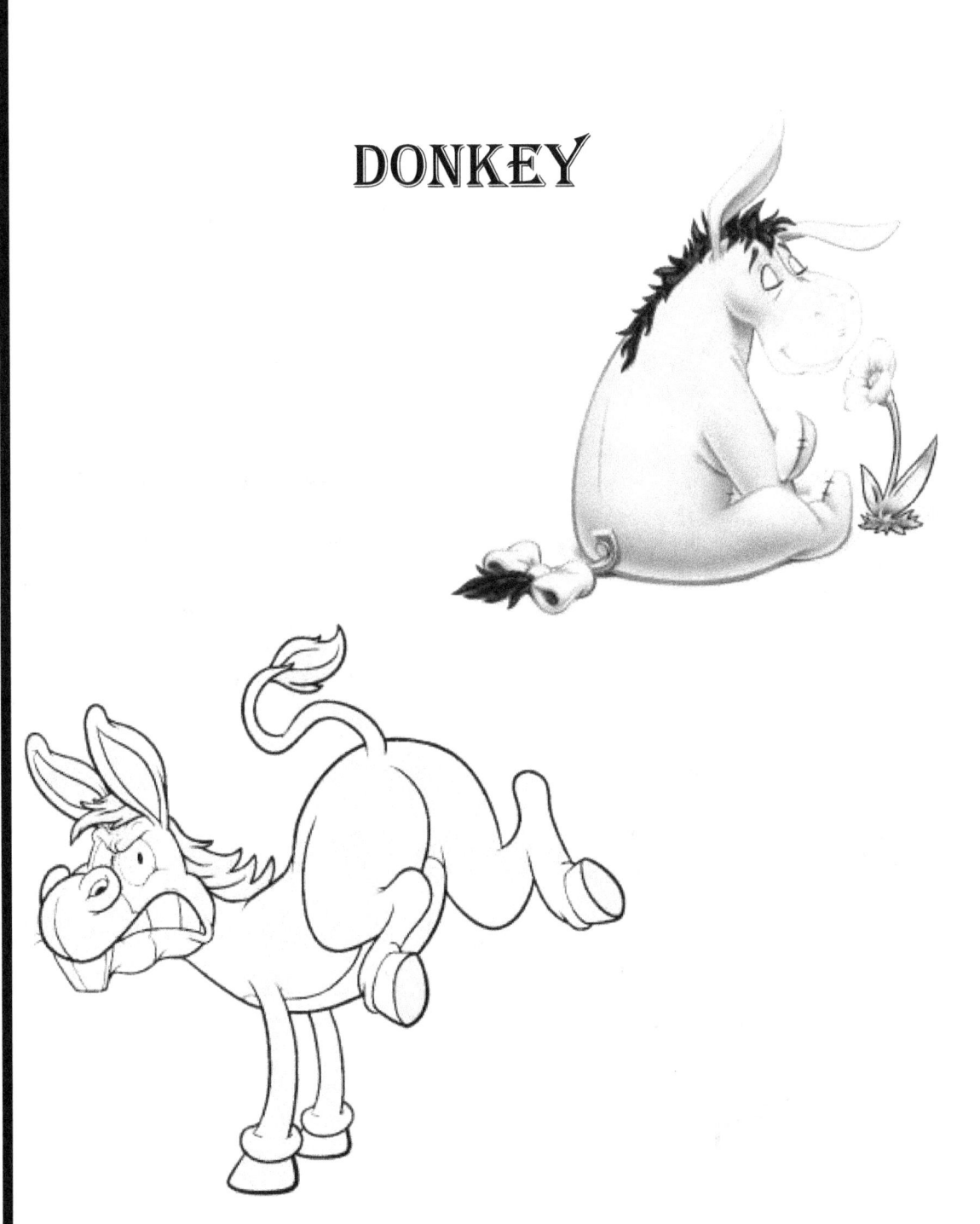

FOX

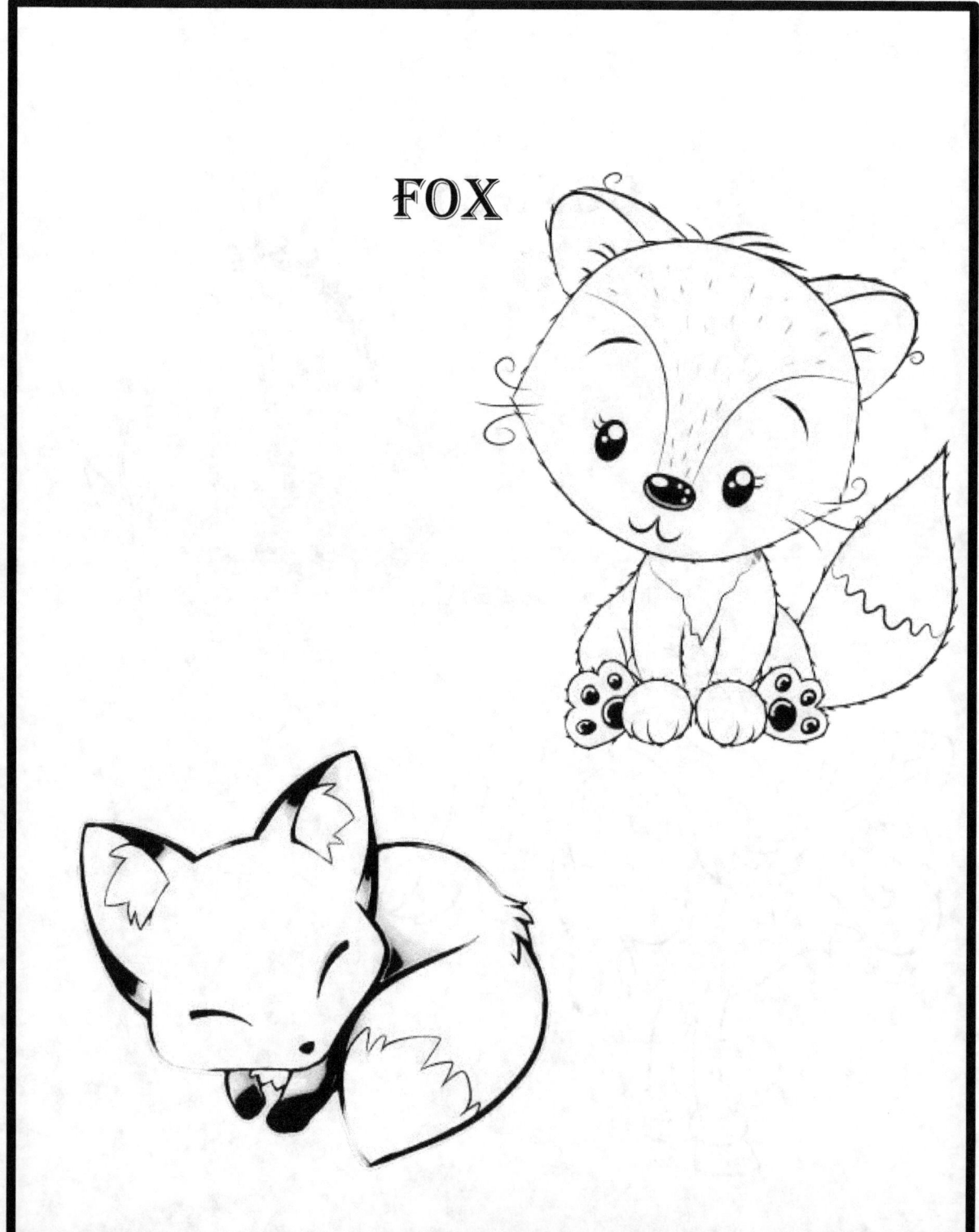

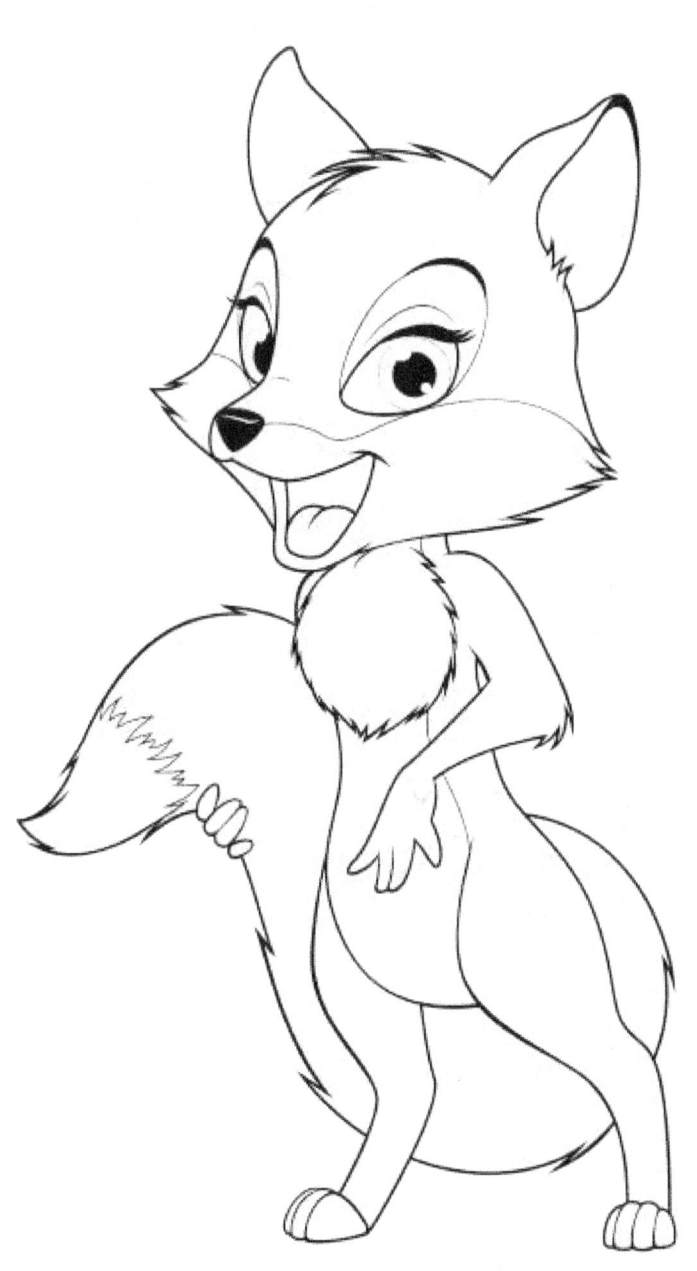

CROCODILE

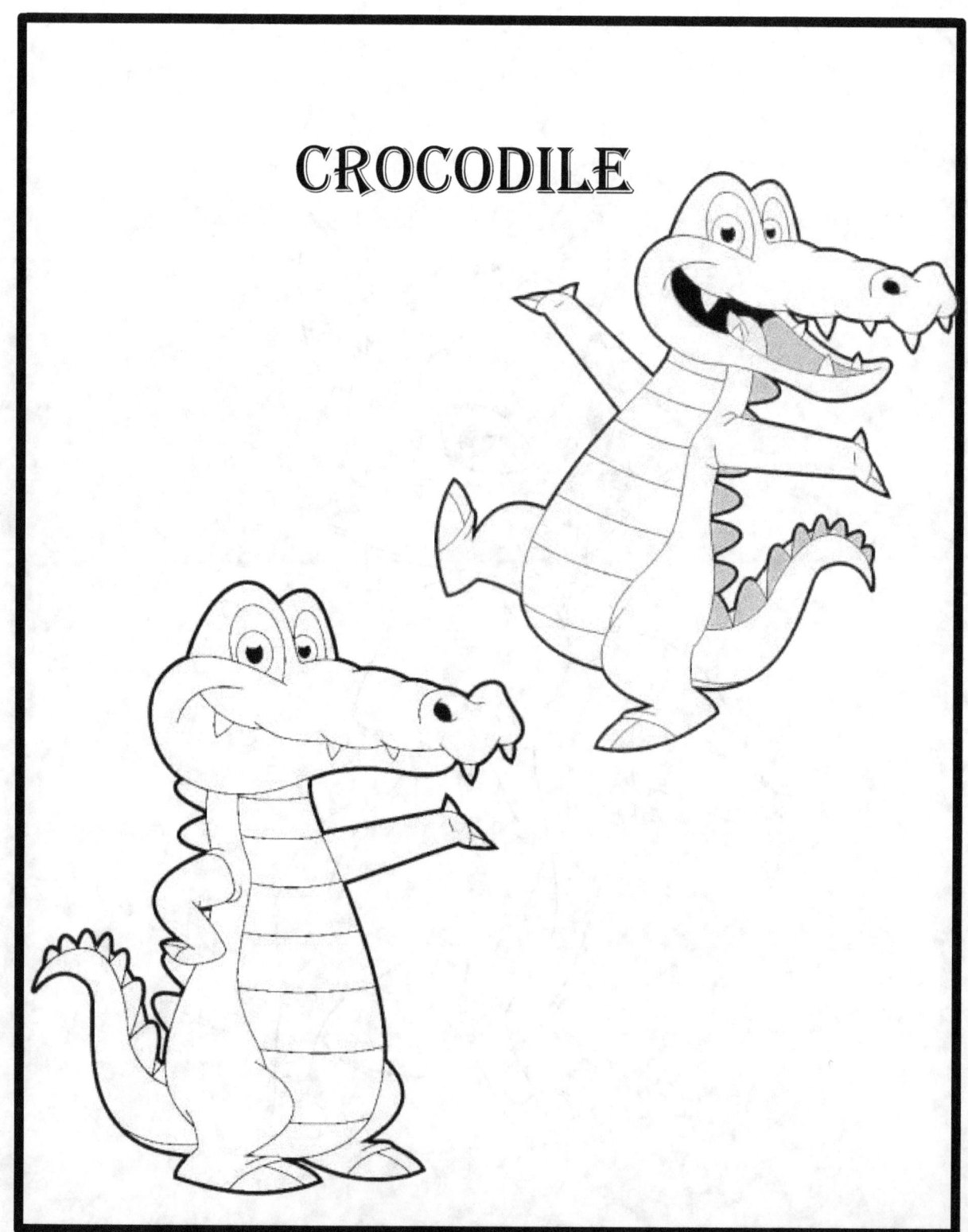

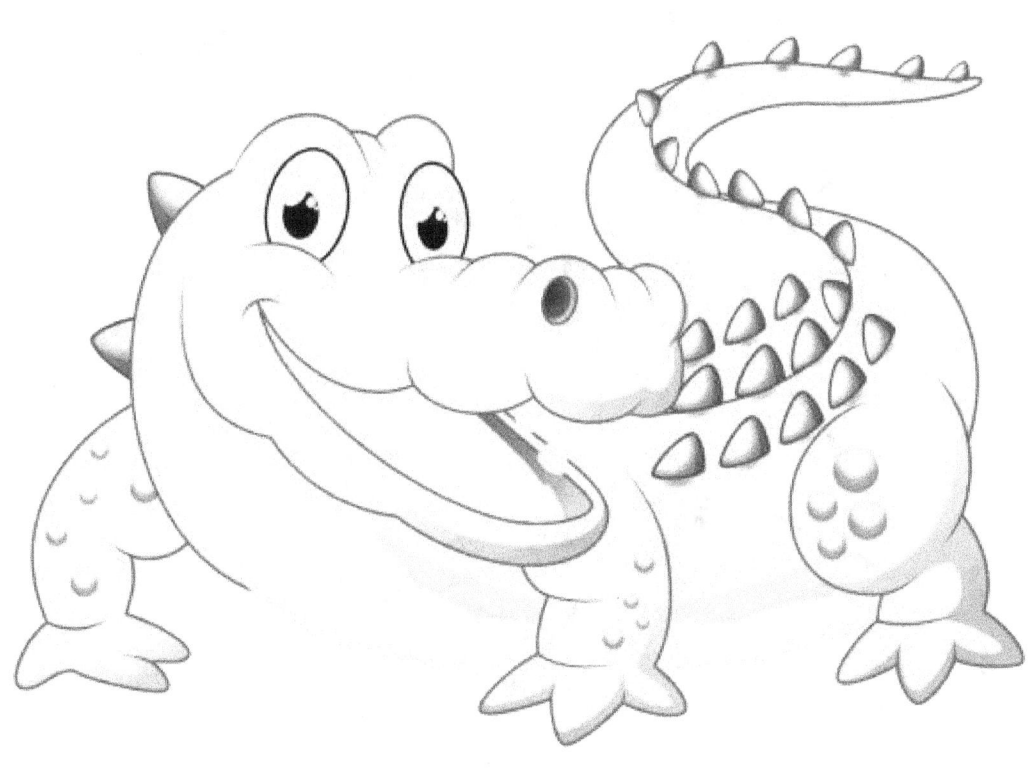

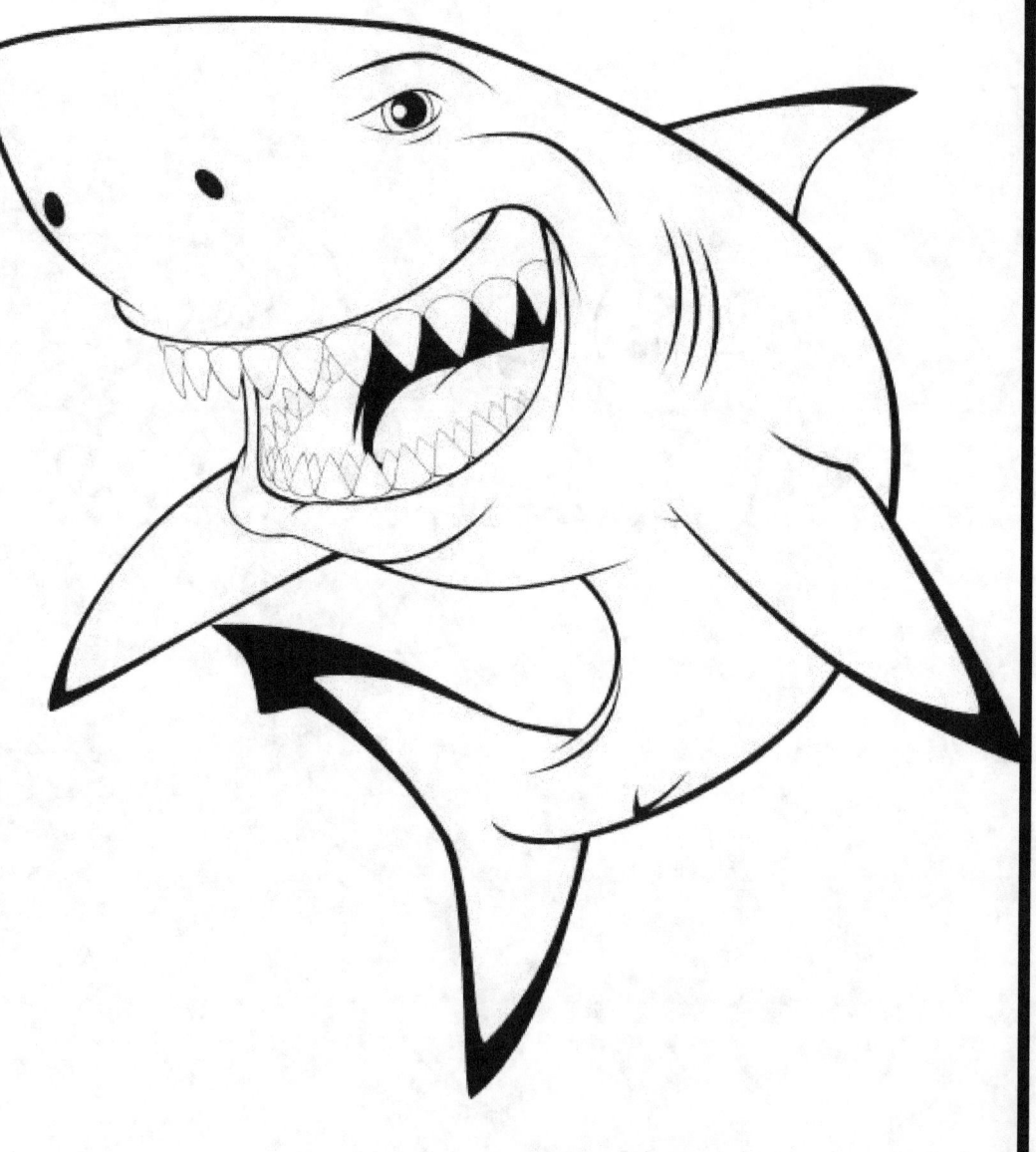

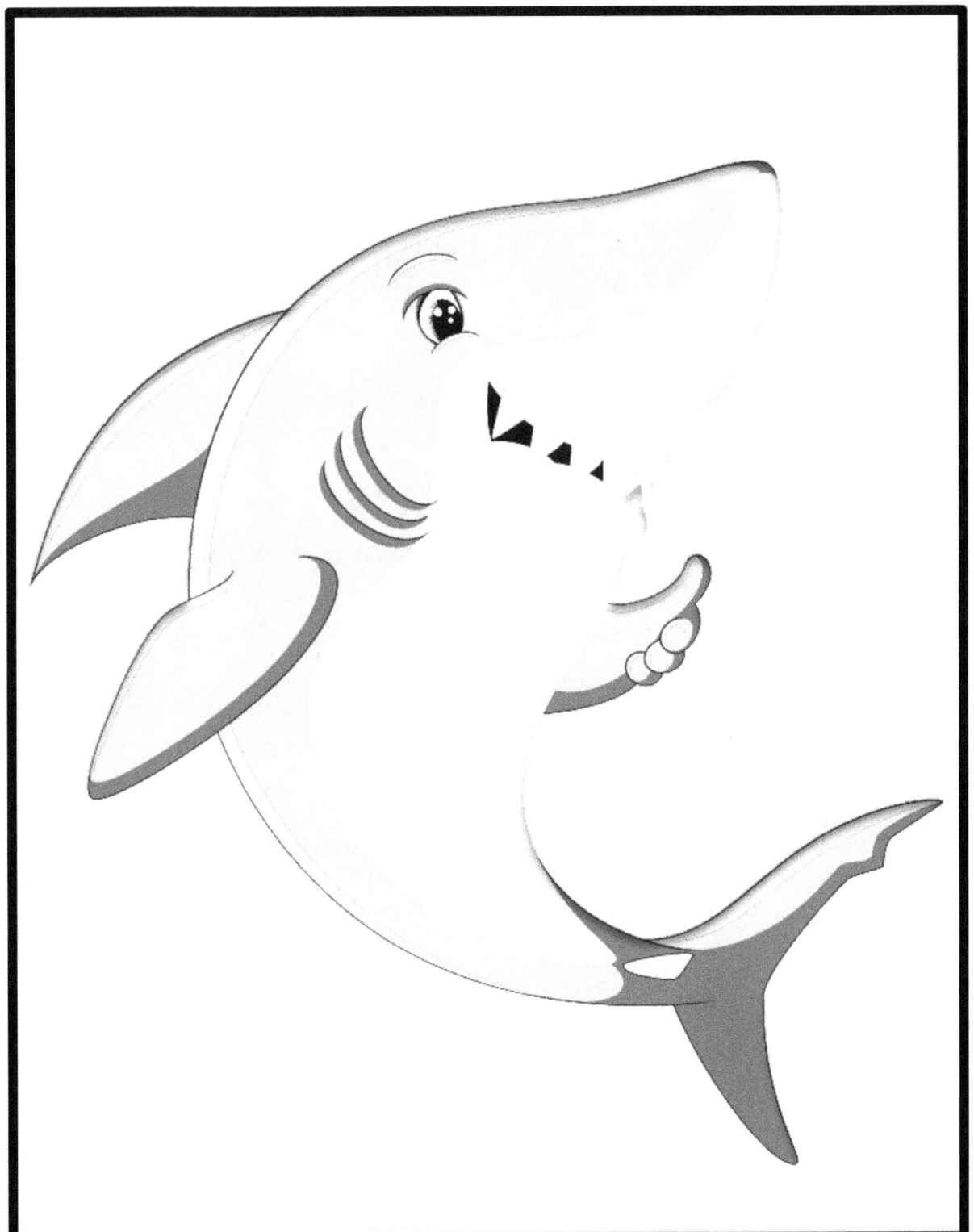

WHITE WHALE

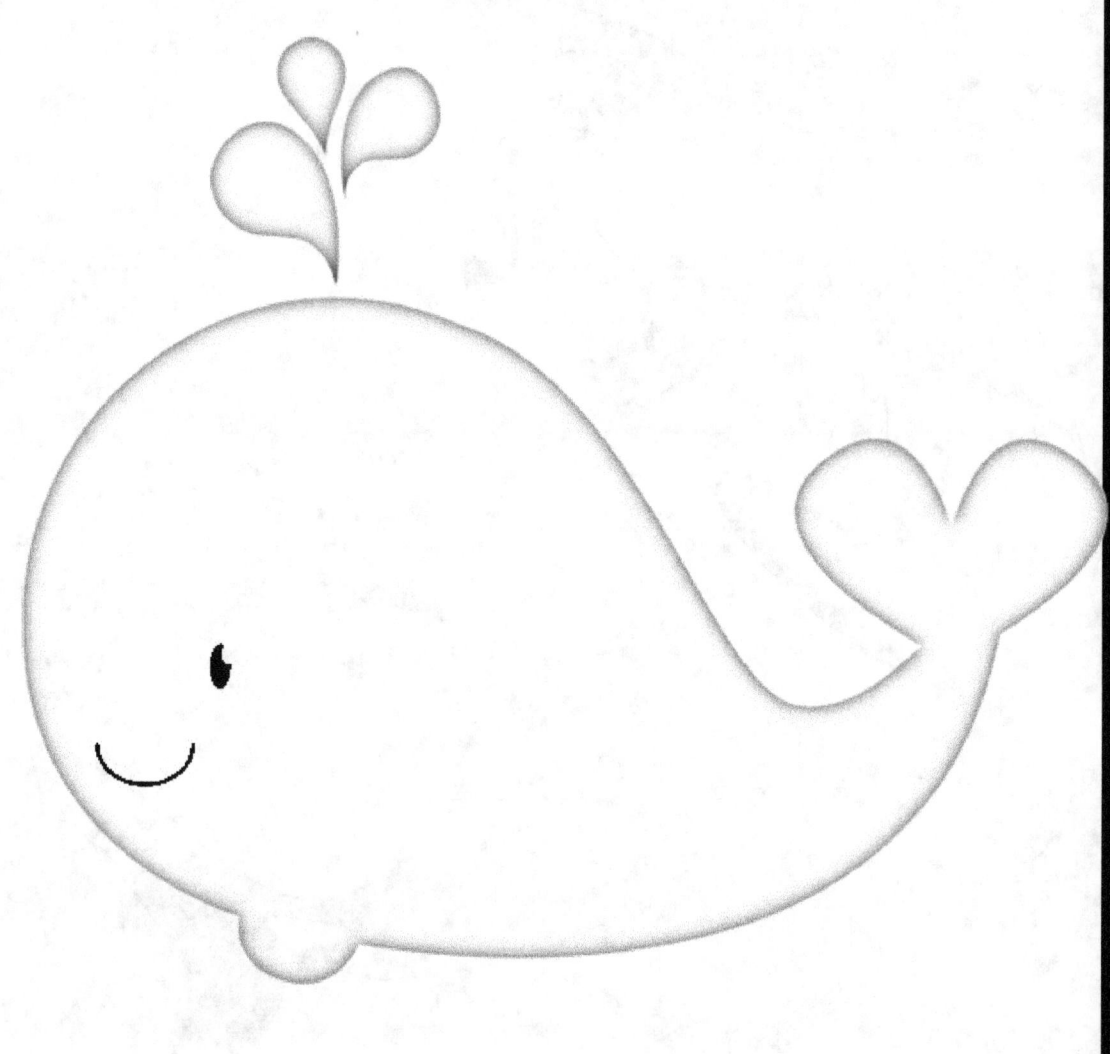

WHALE

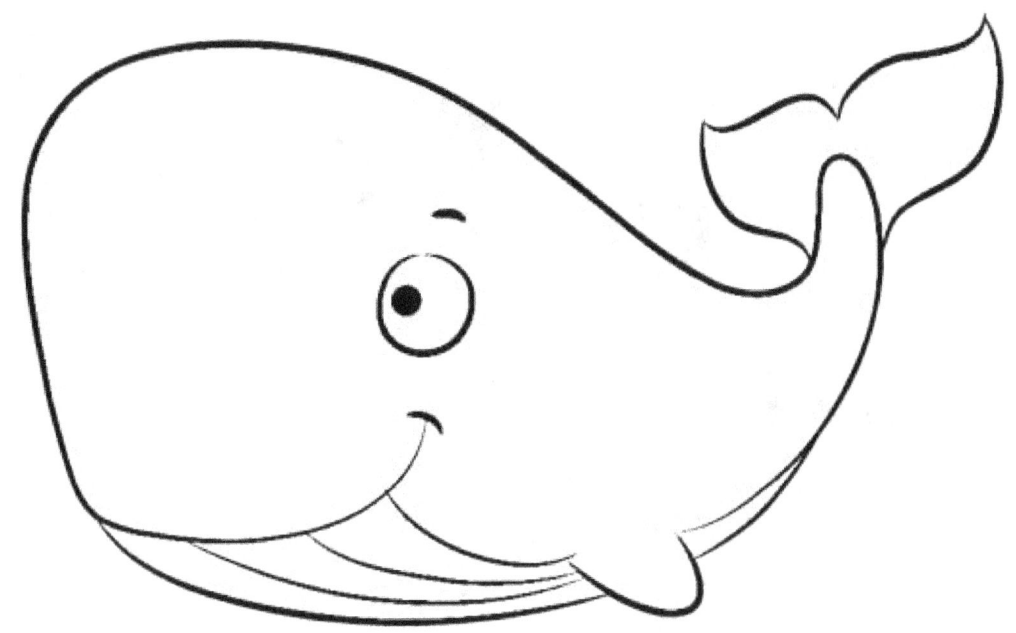

FISH

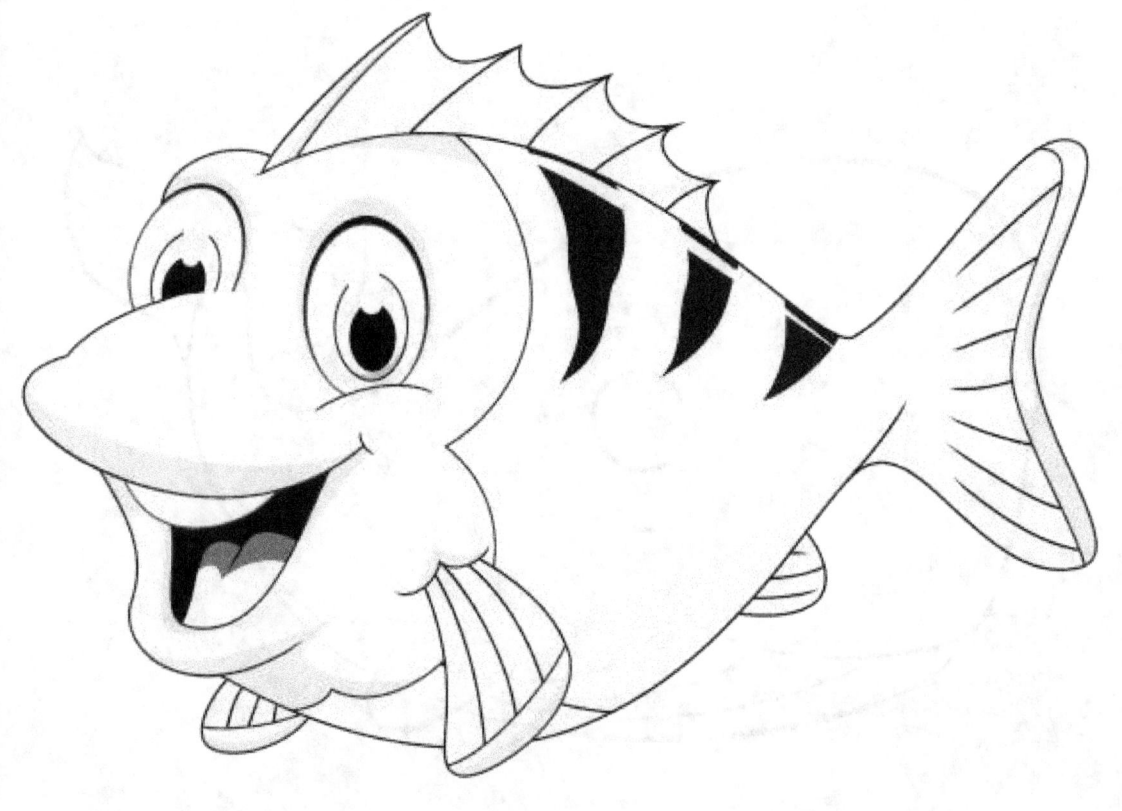

TORTOISE

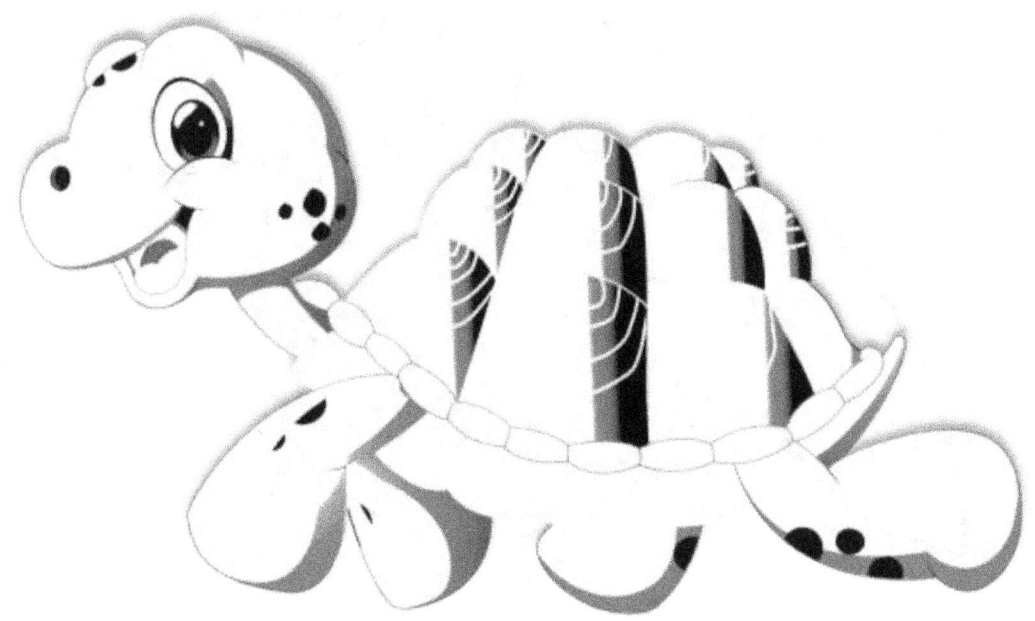

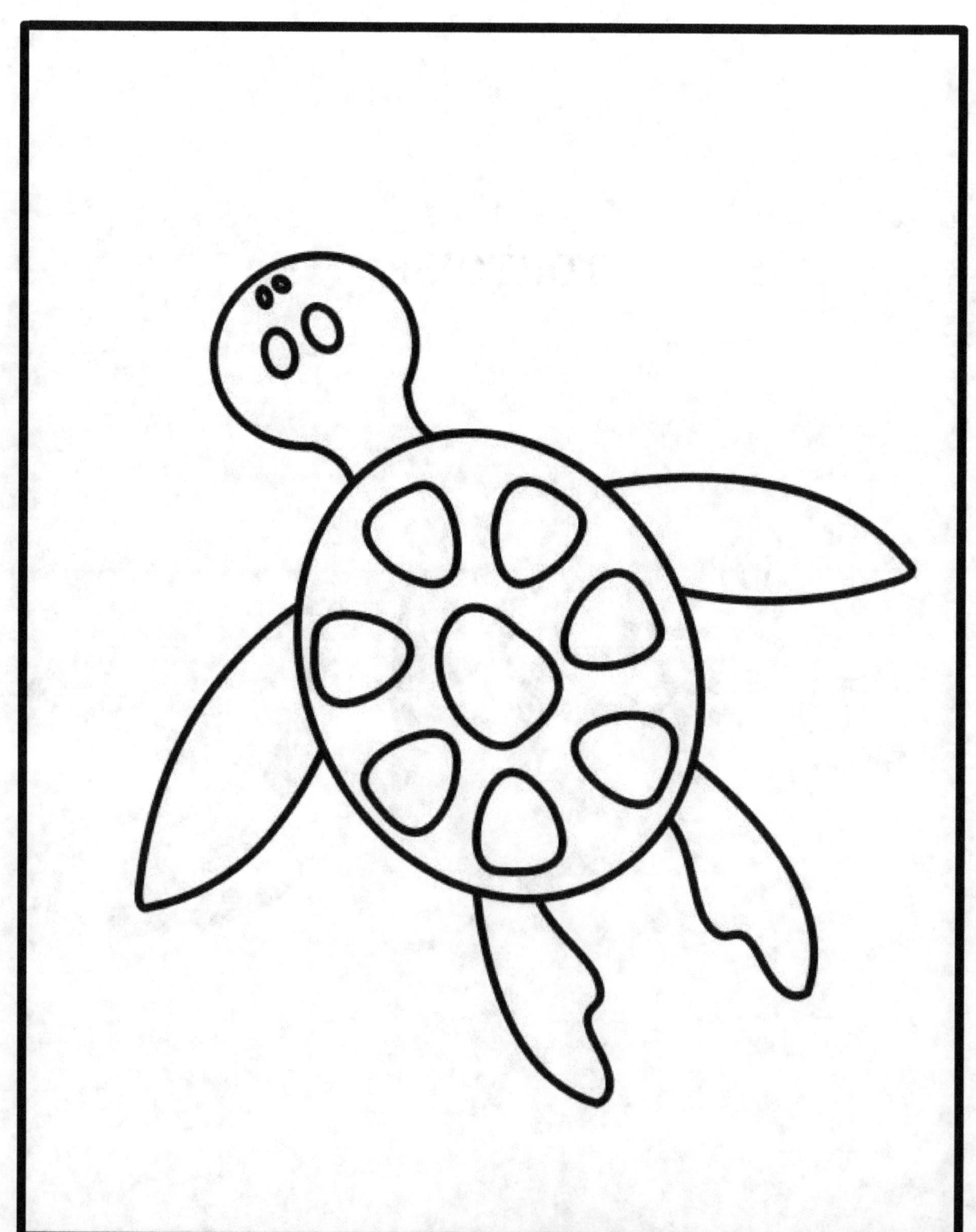

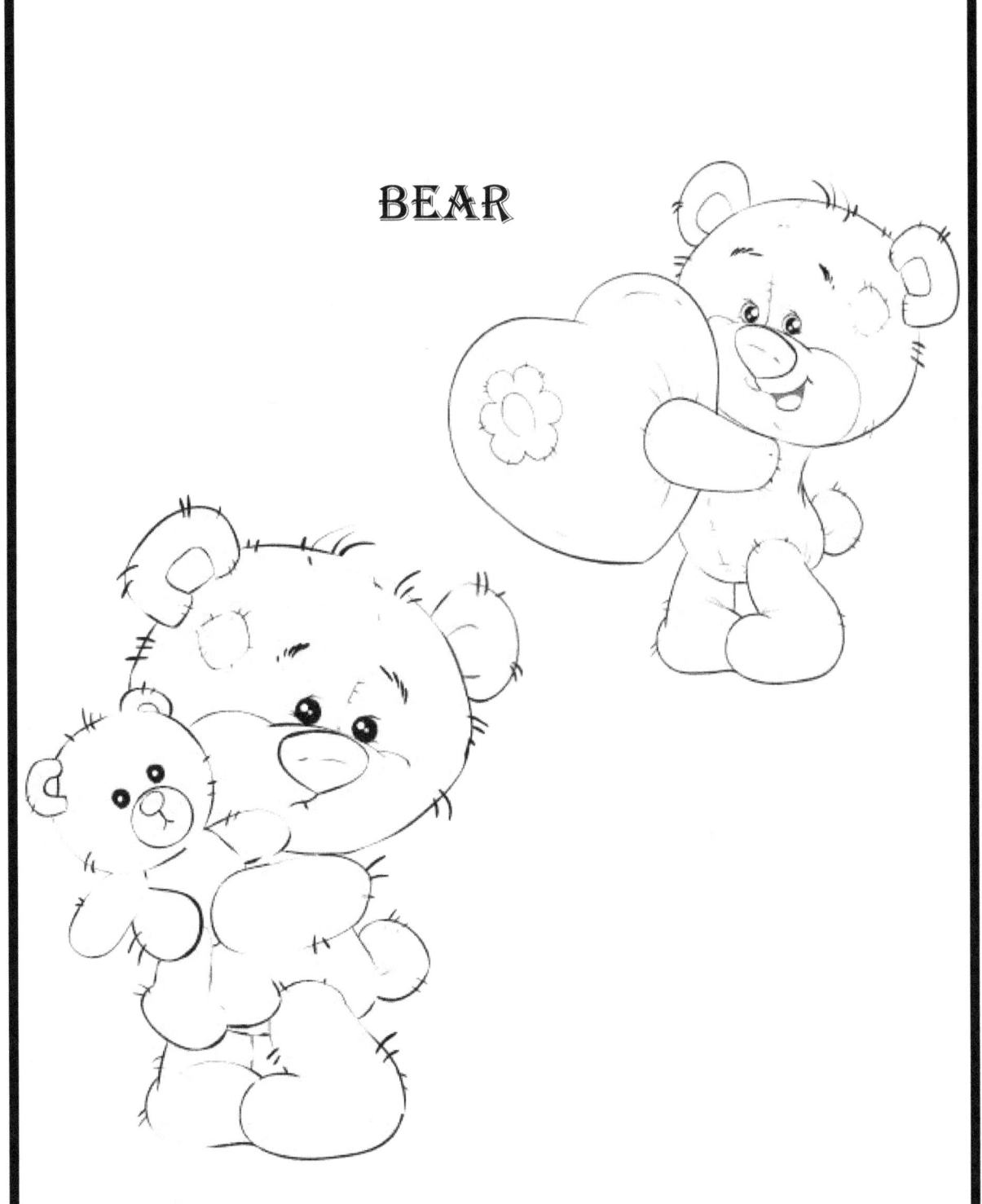

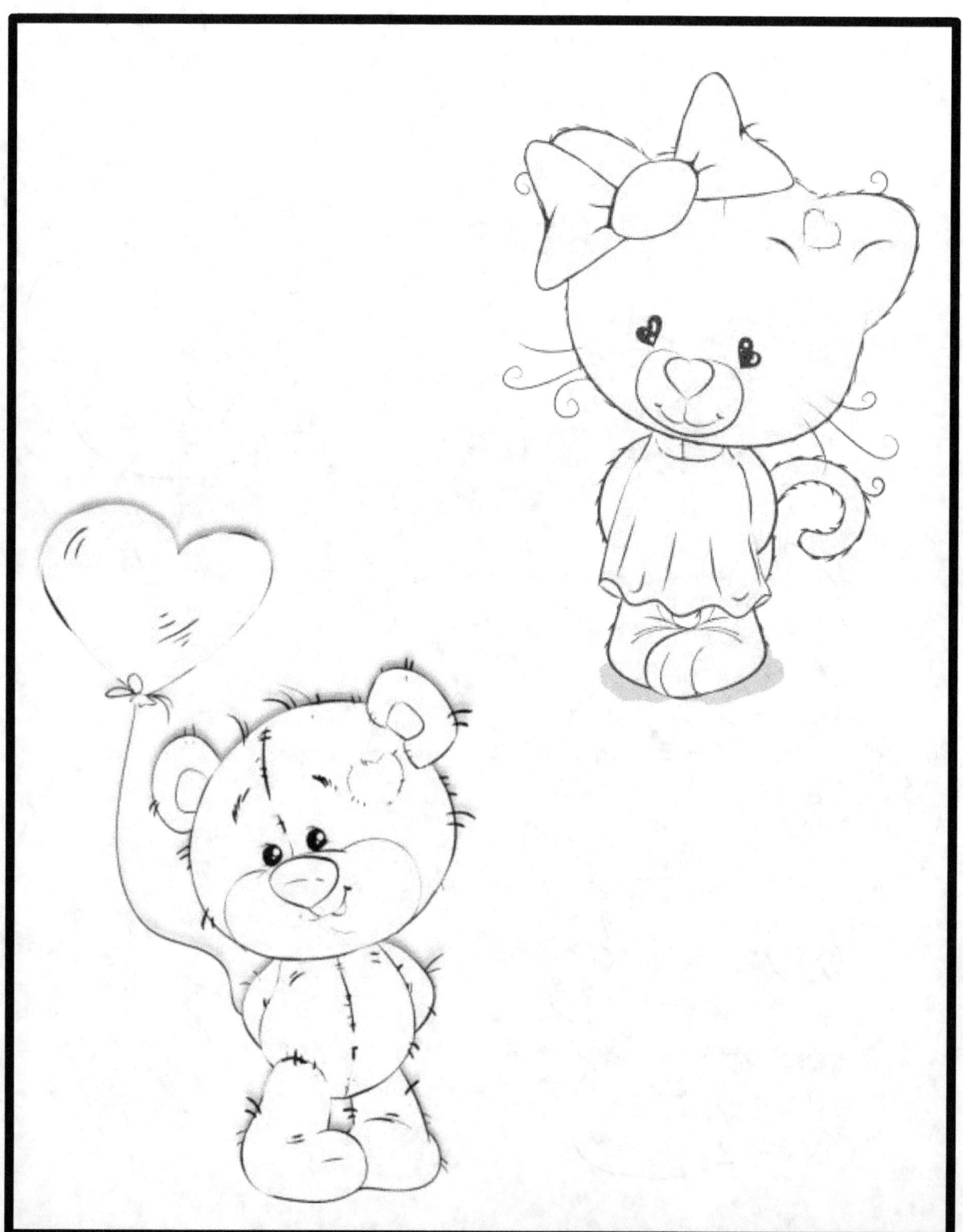

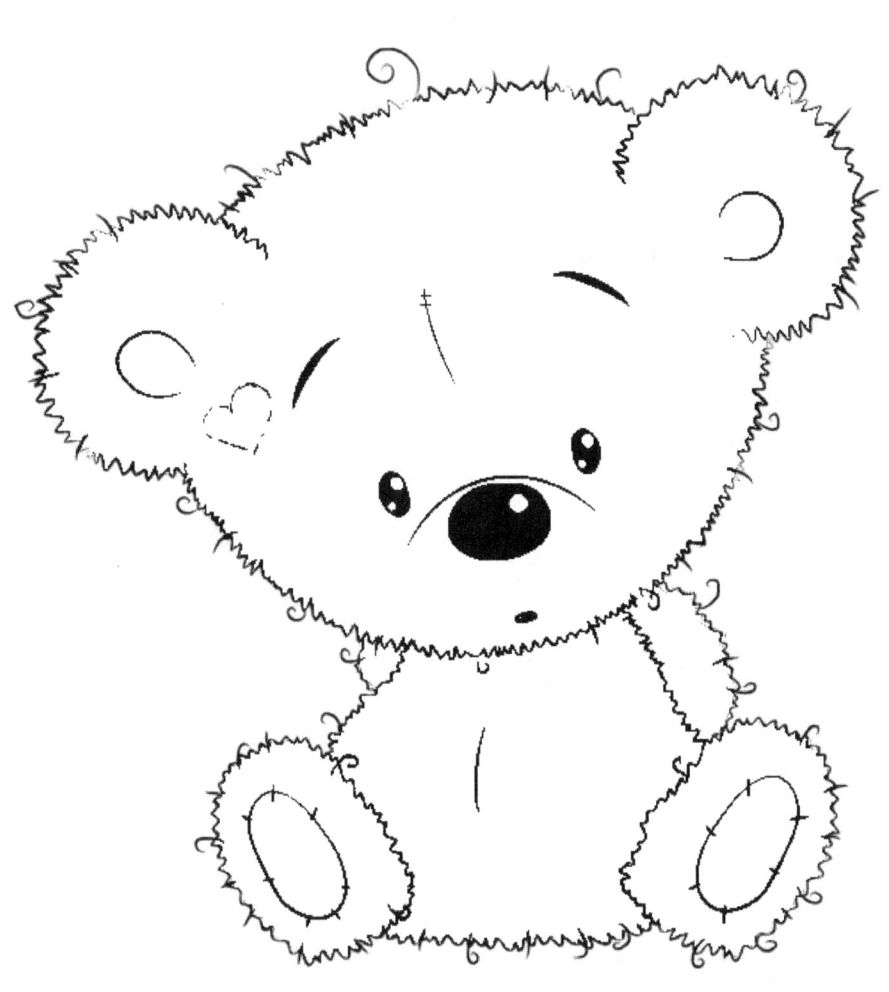

WHITE BEAR

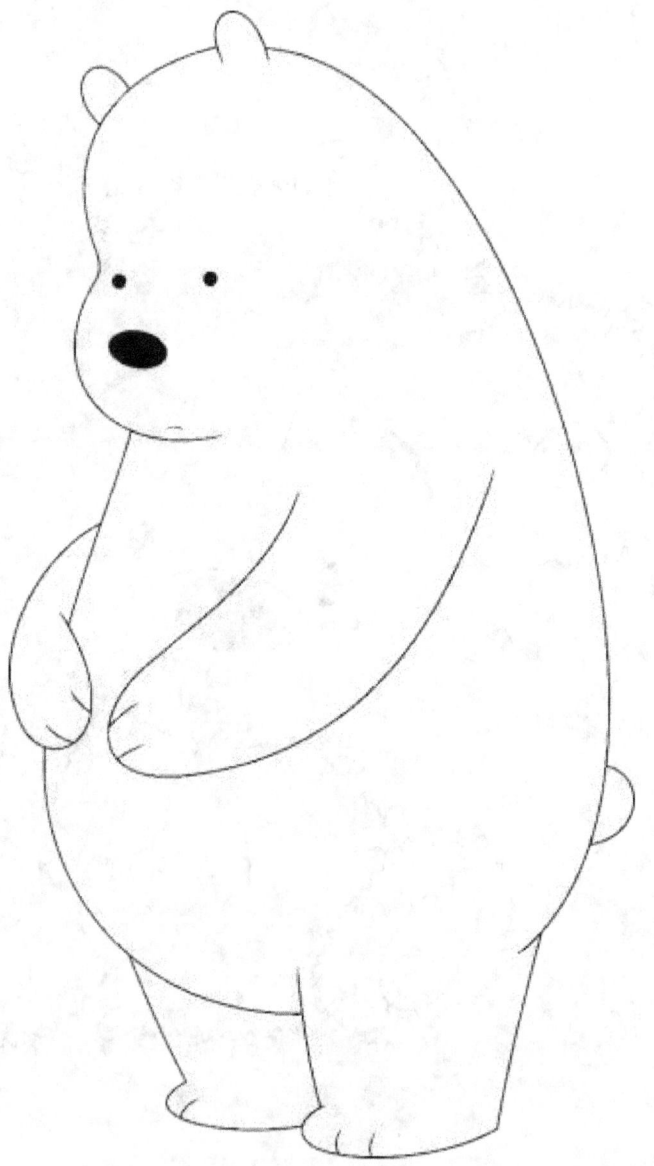

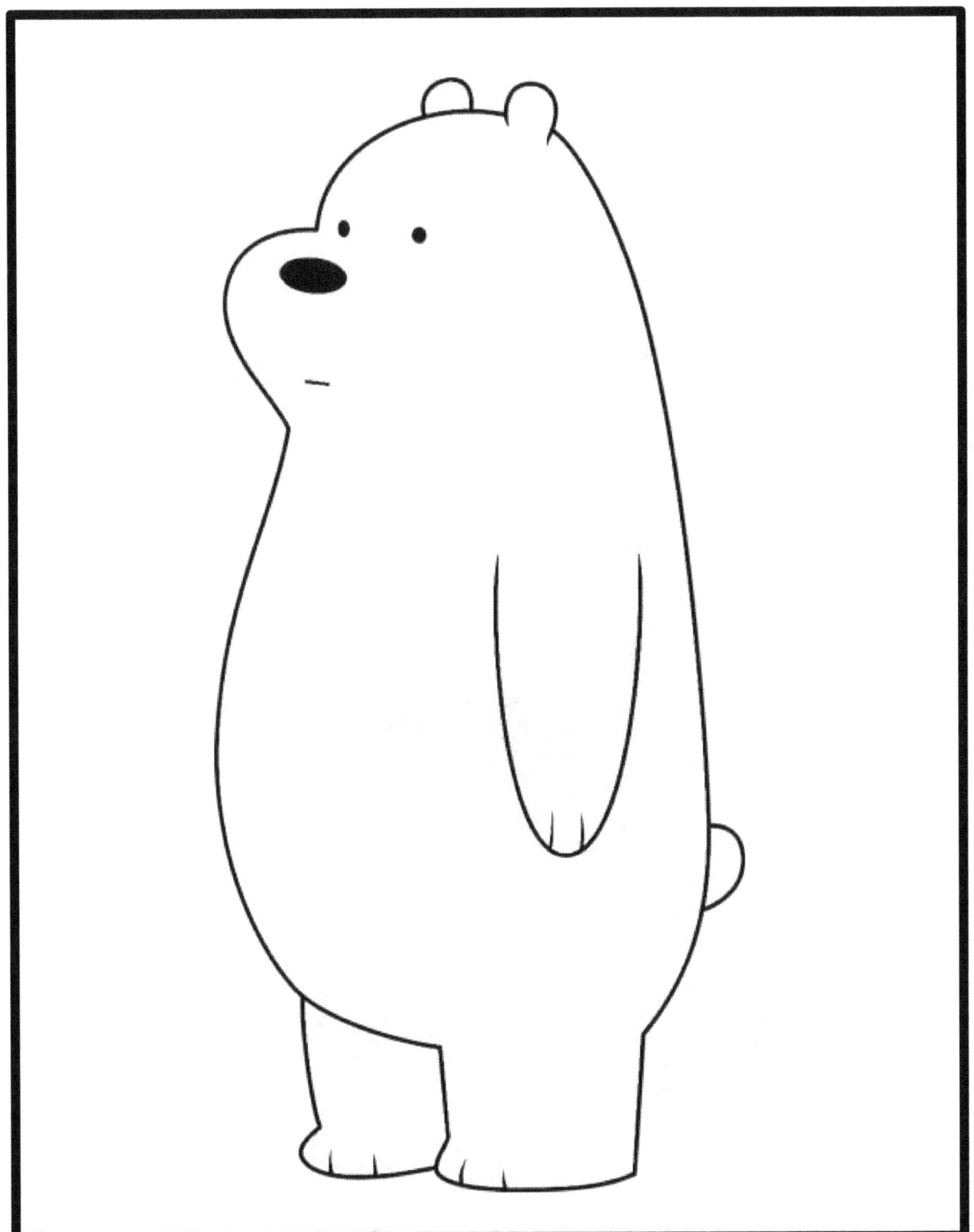

KOALA

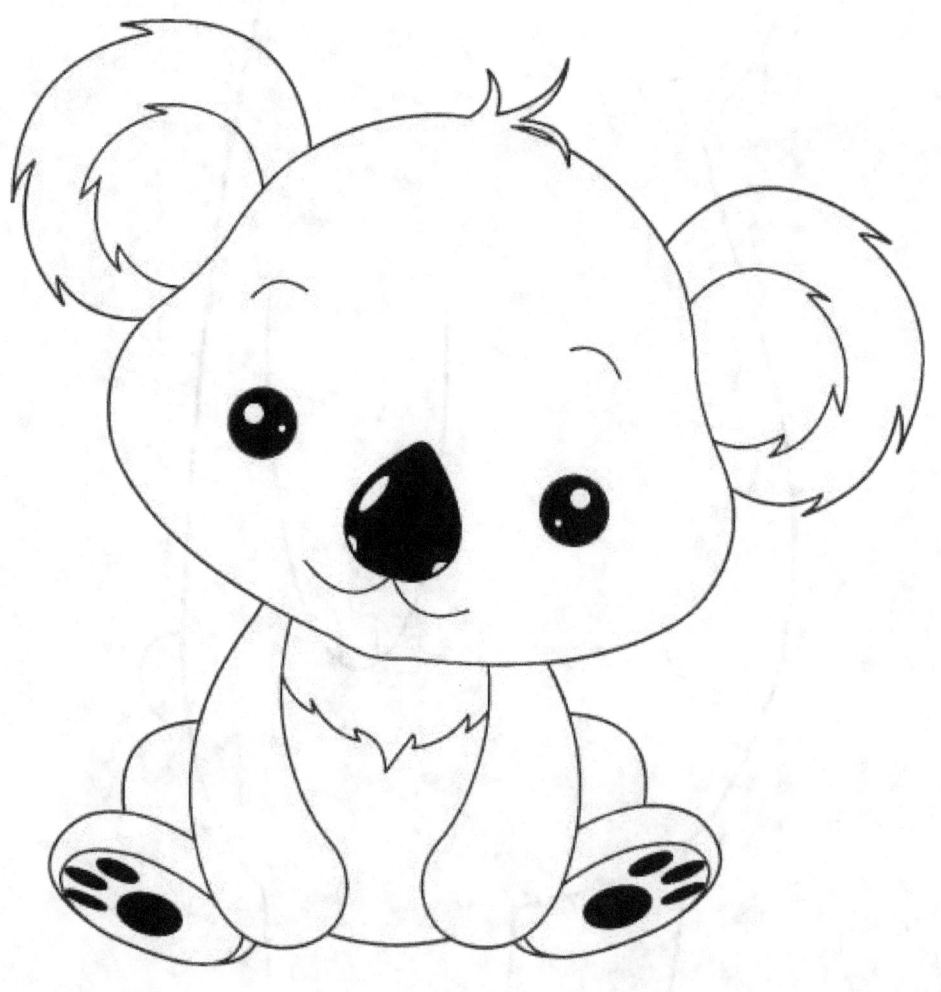

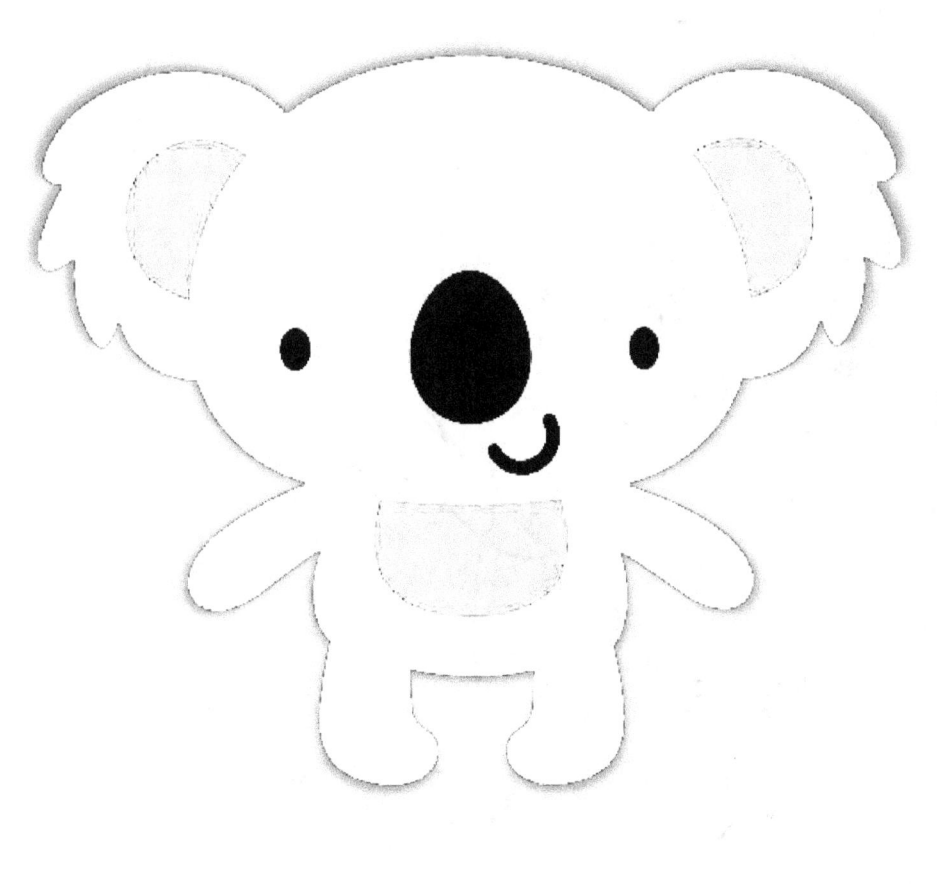

RHINO

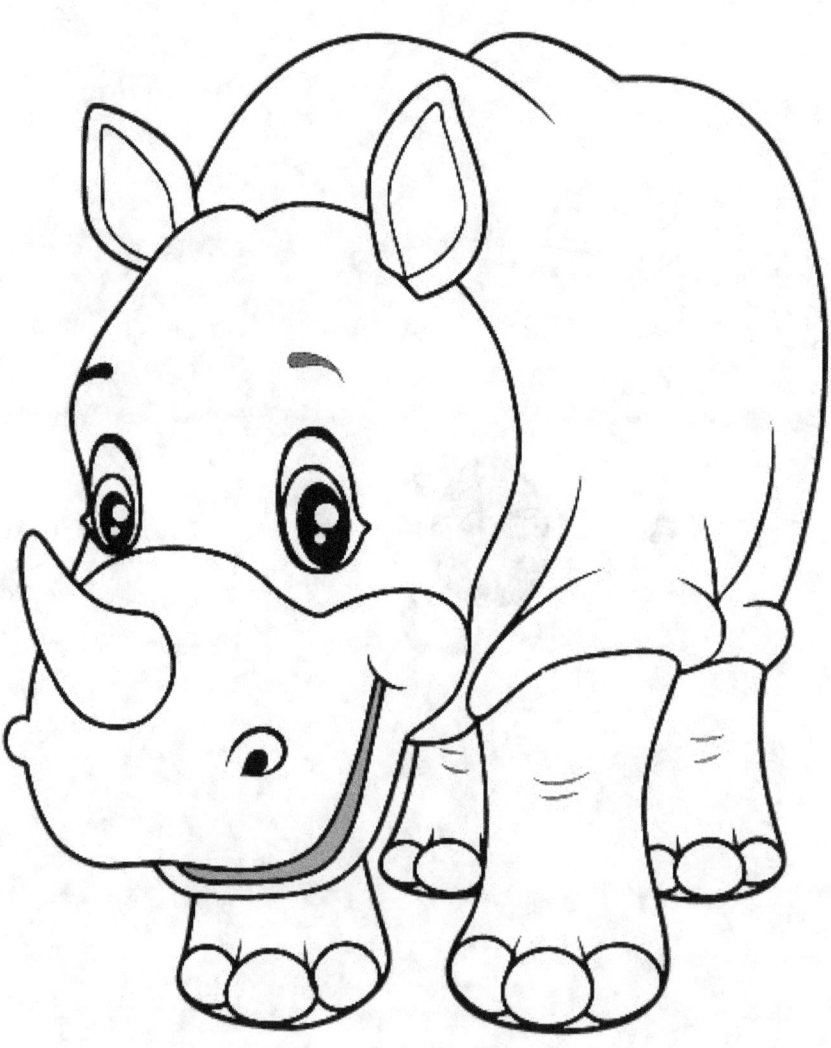

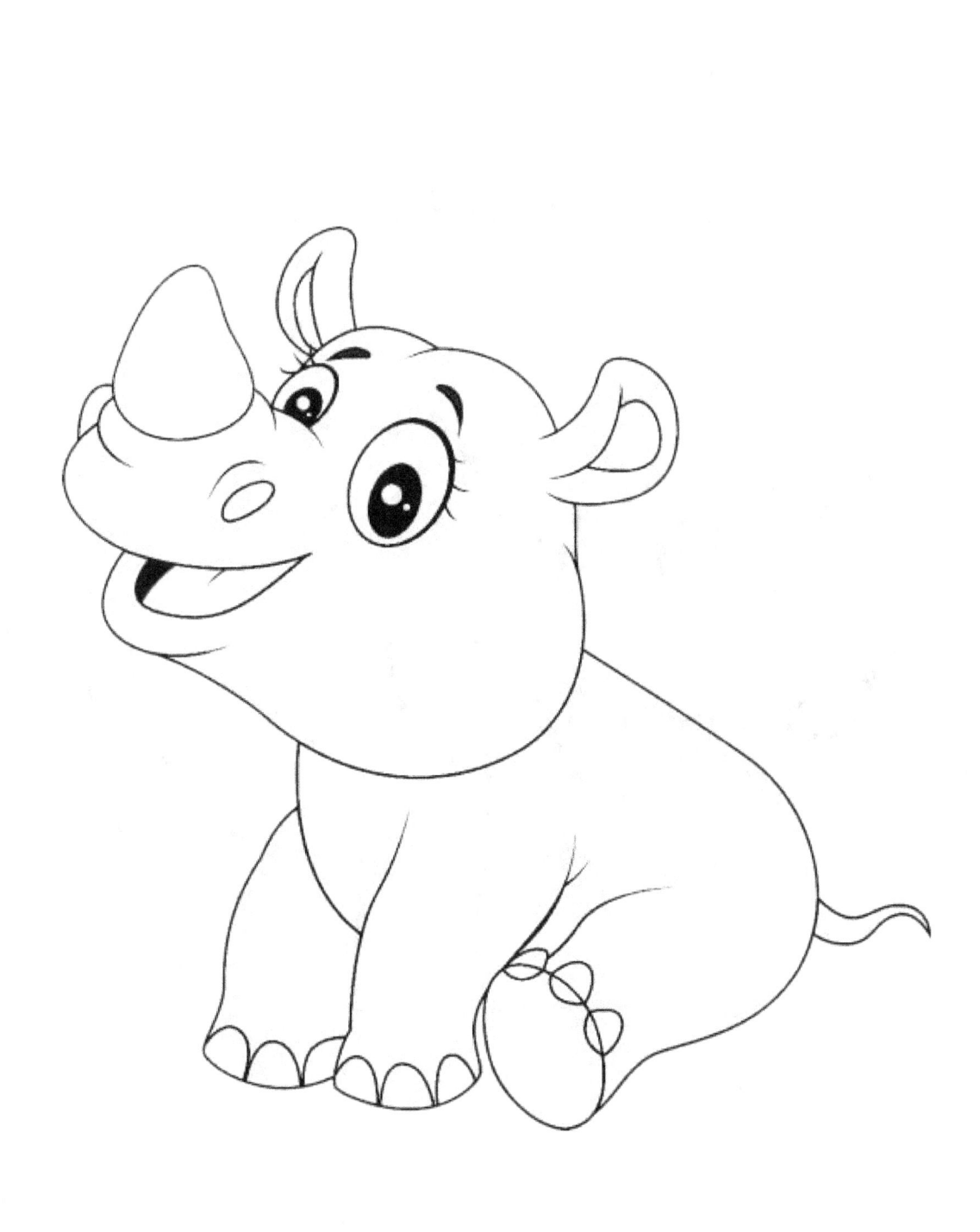

HIPPOPOTAMUS

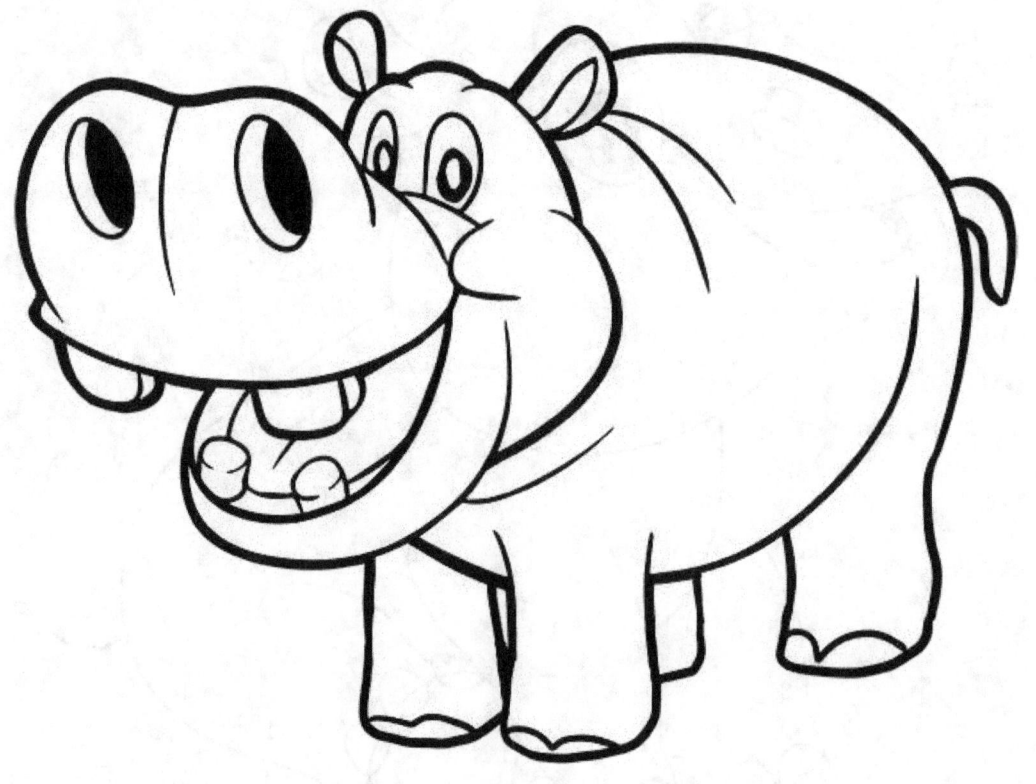

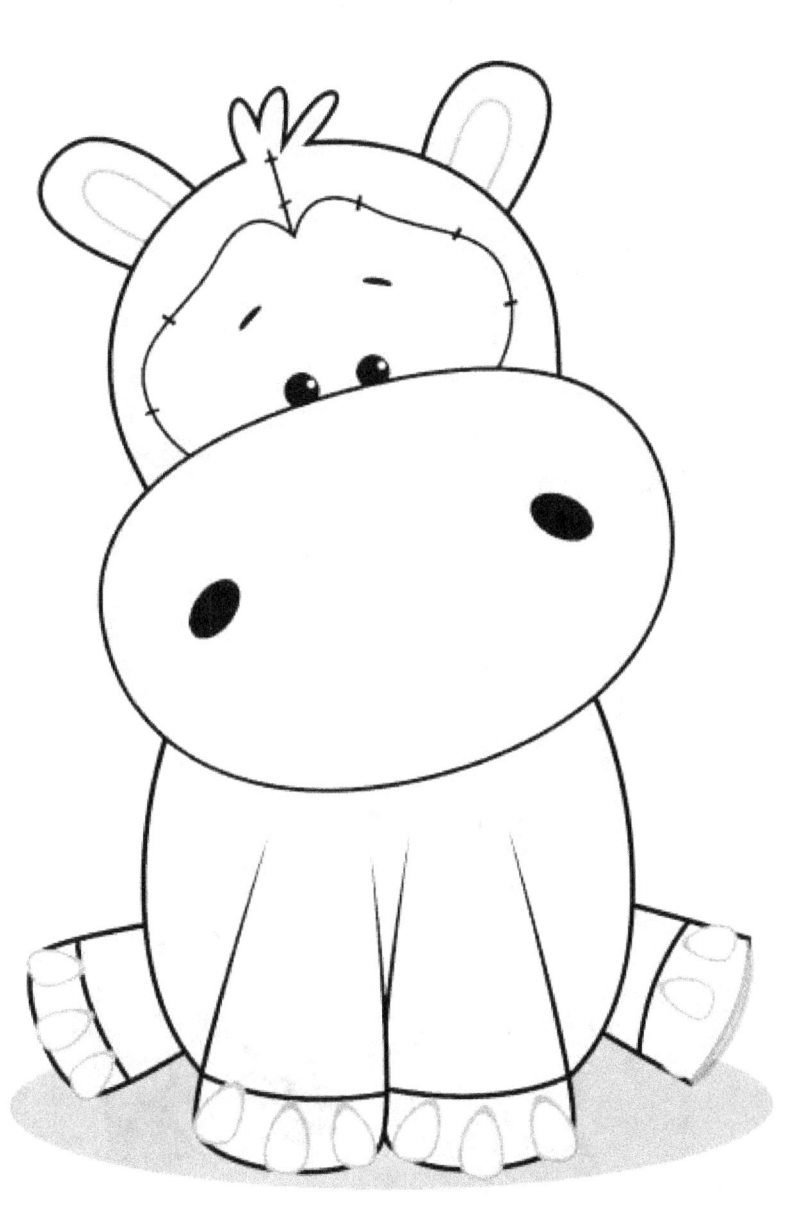

GOAT

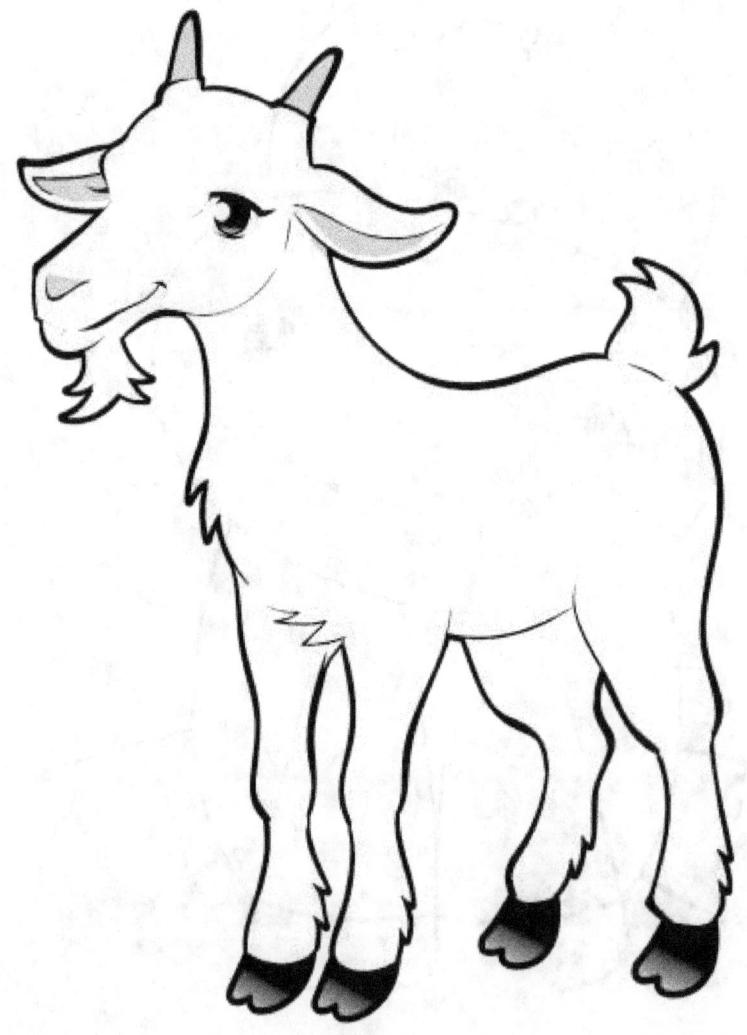

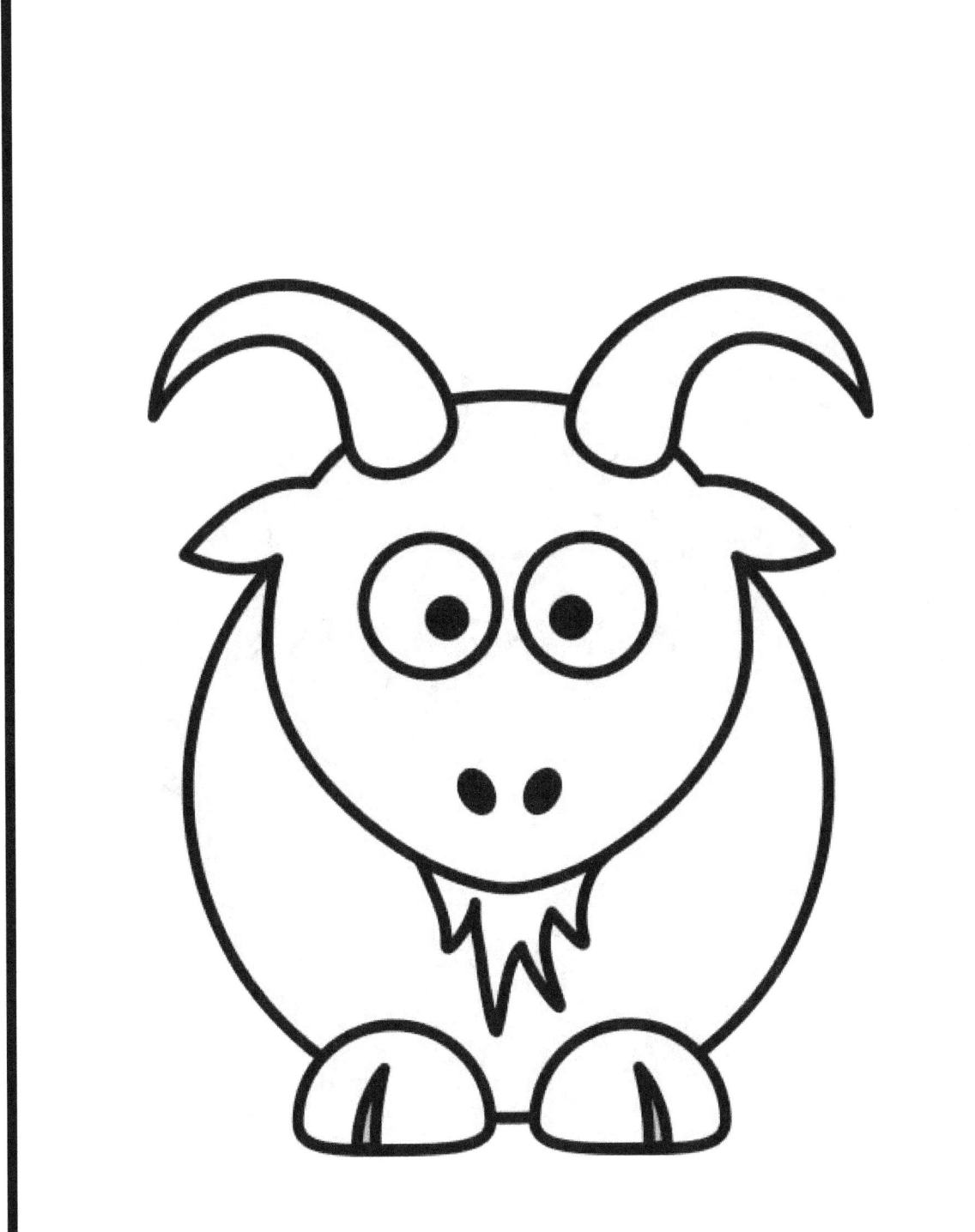

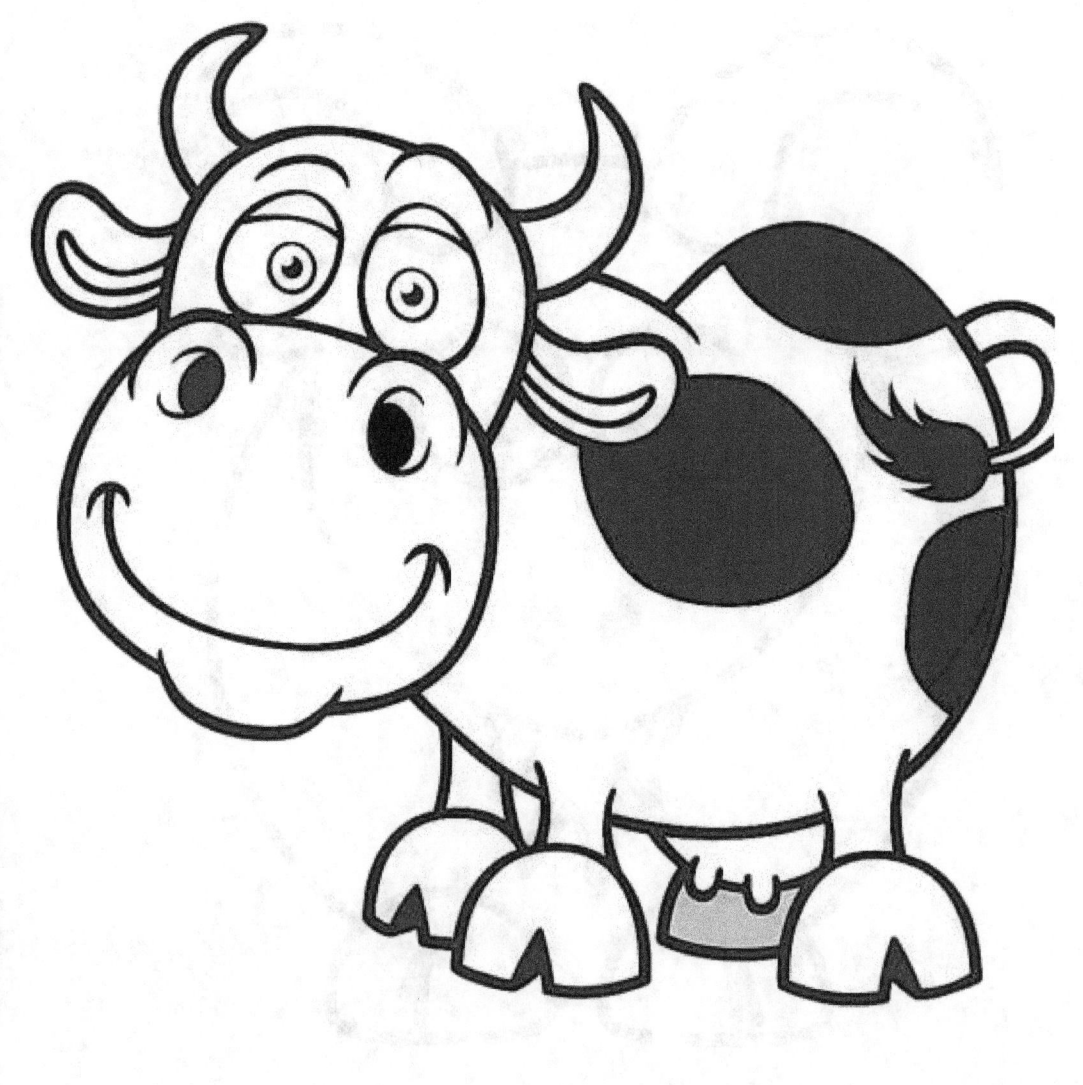

PIG

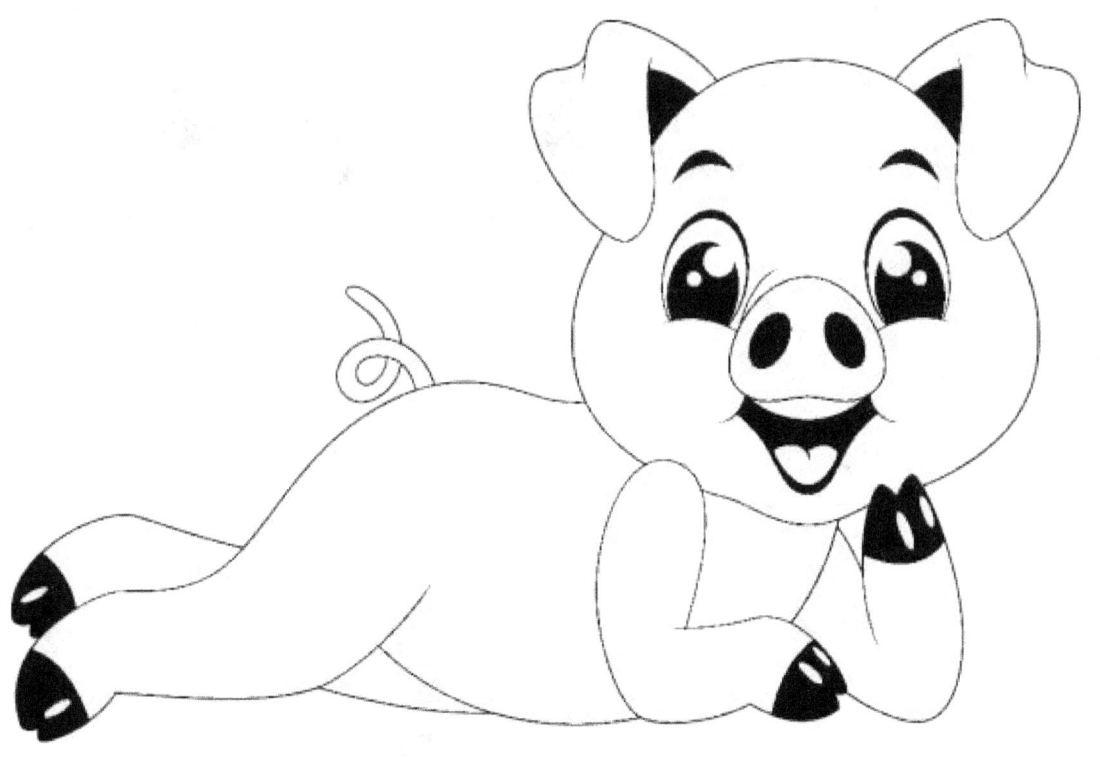

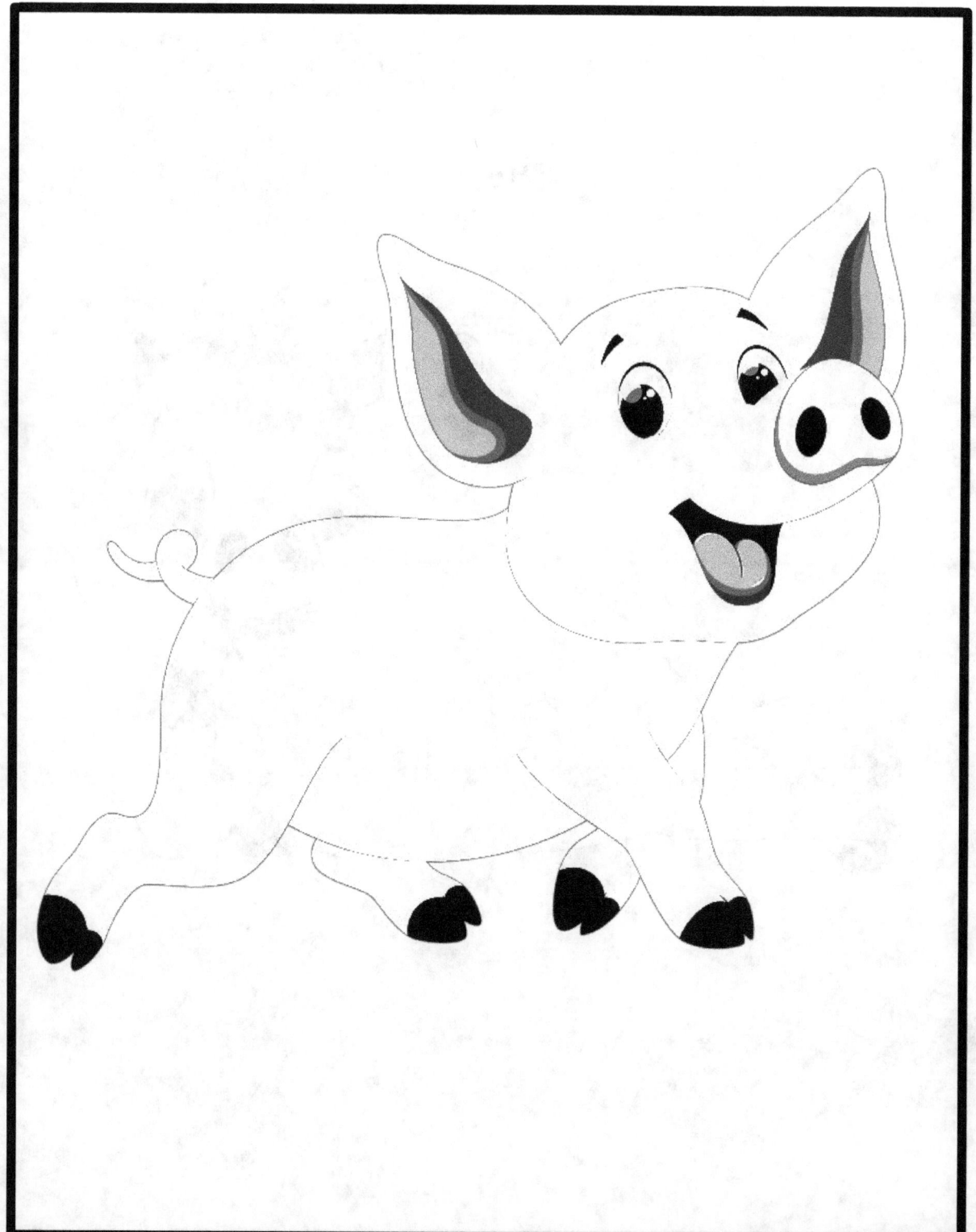

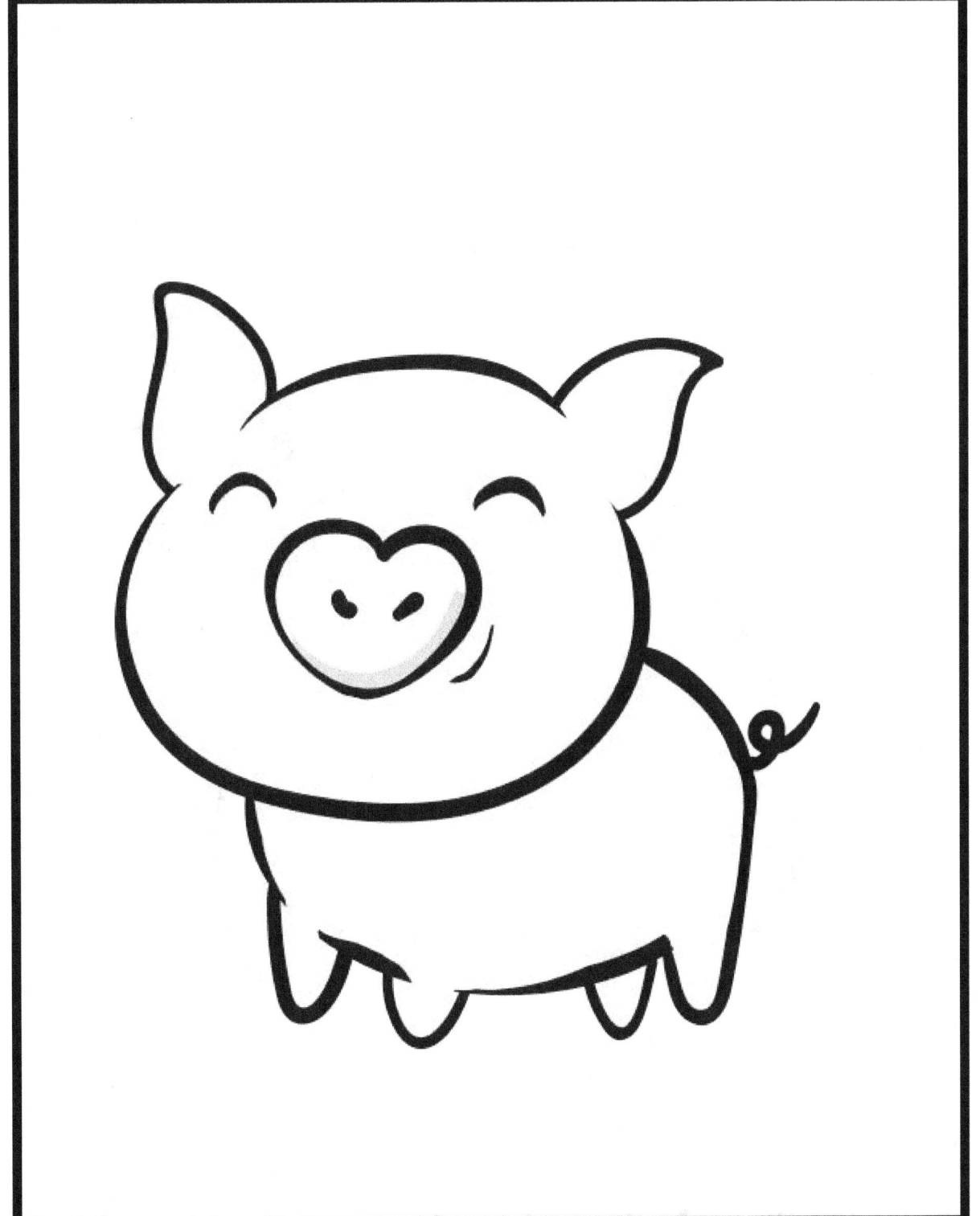

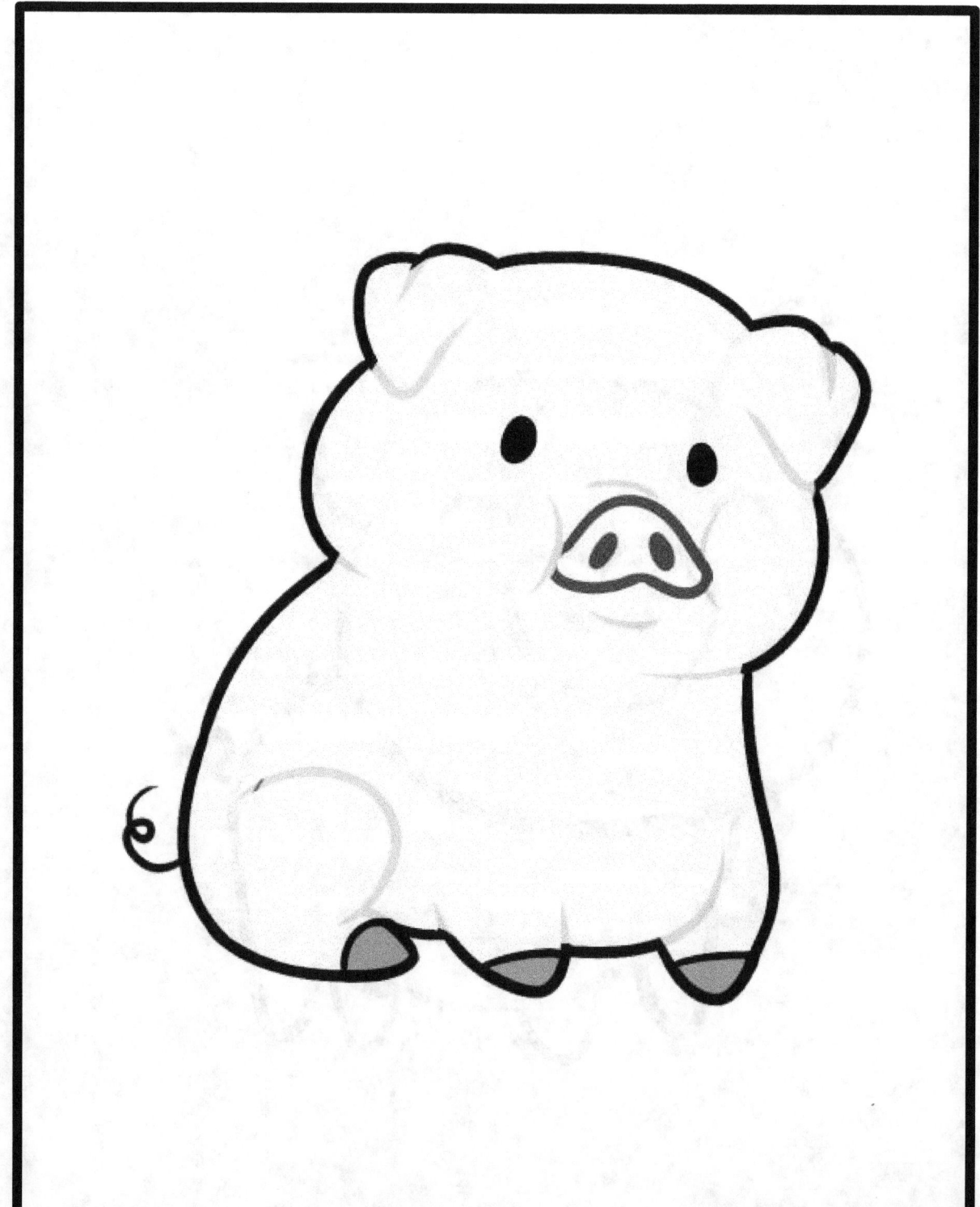

MONKEY

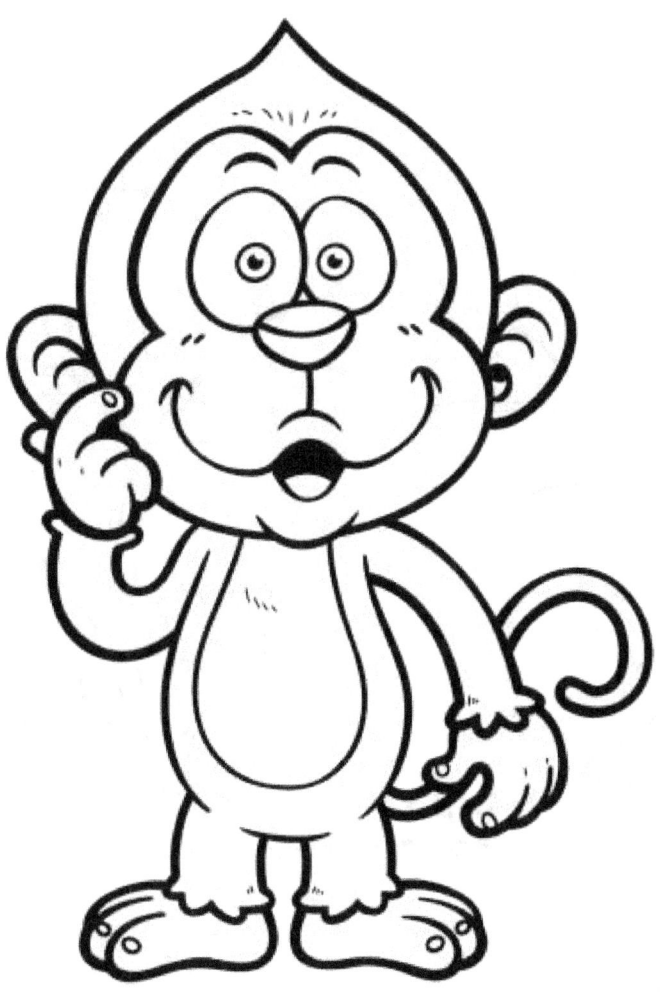

SNAIL

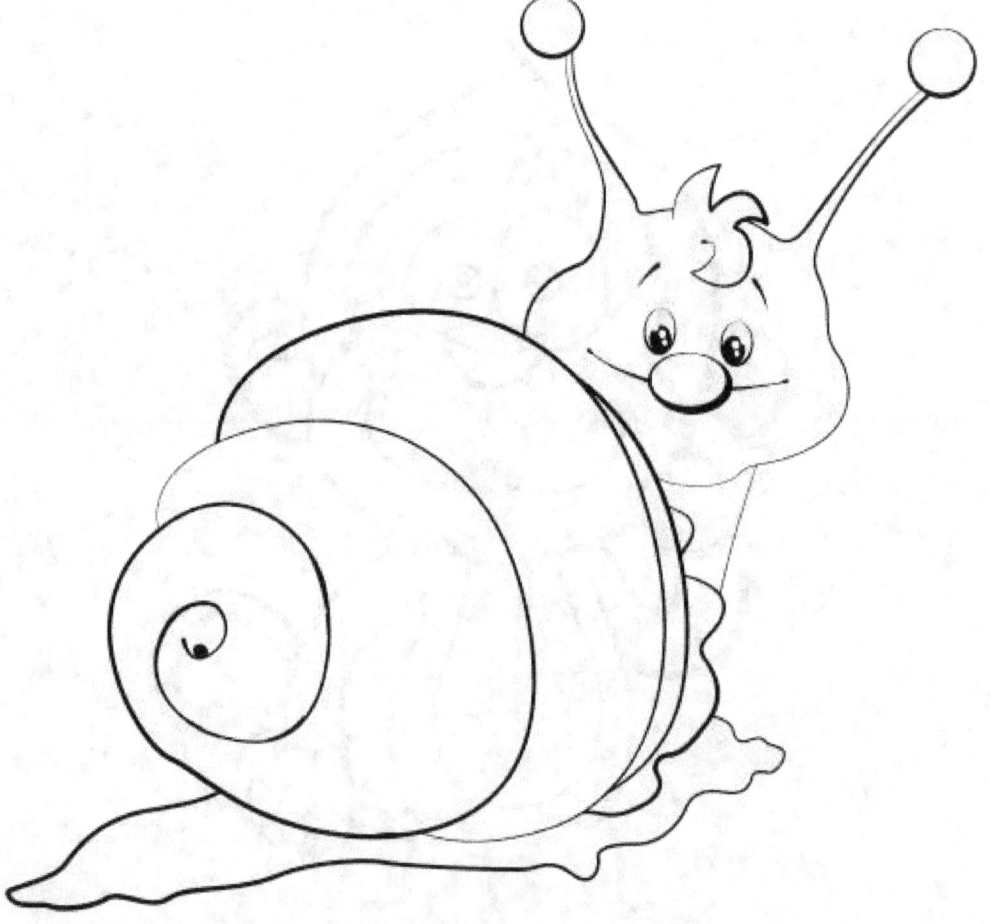

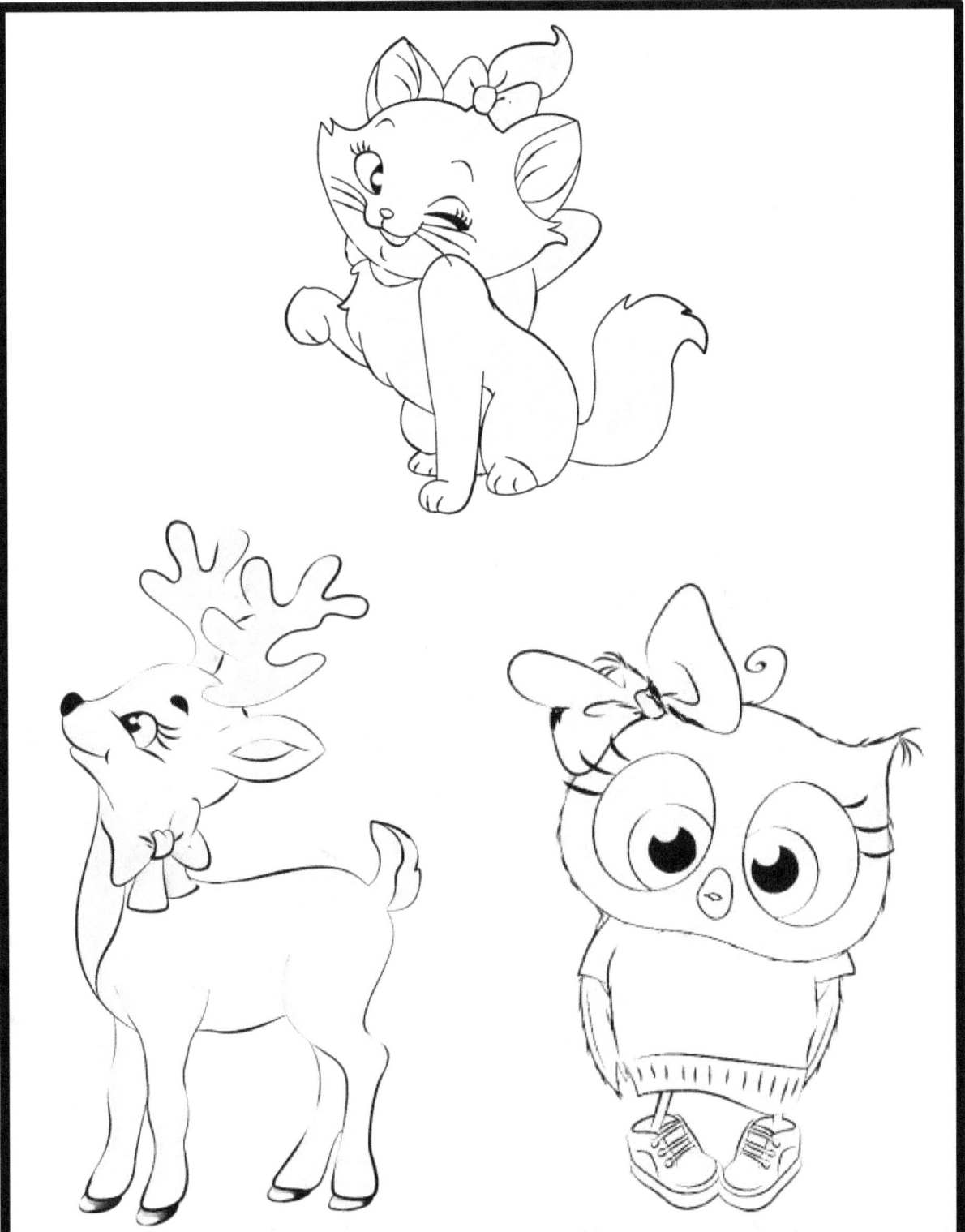

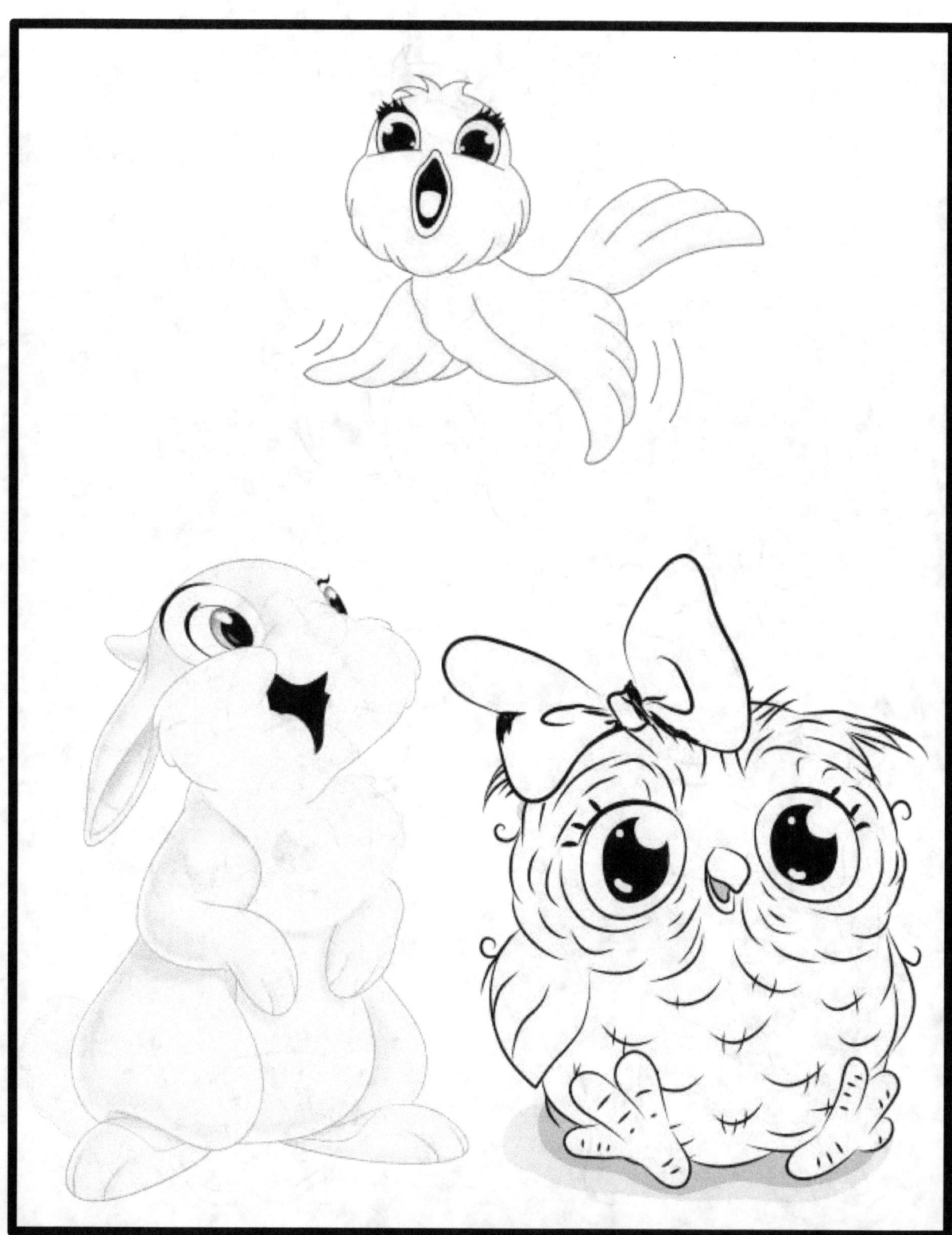

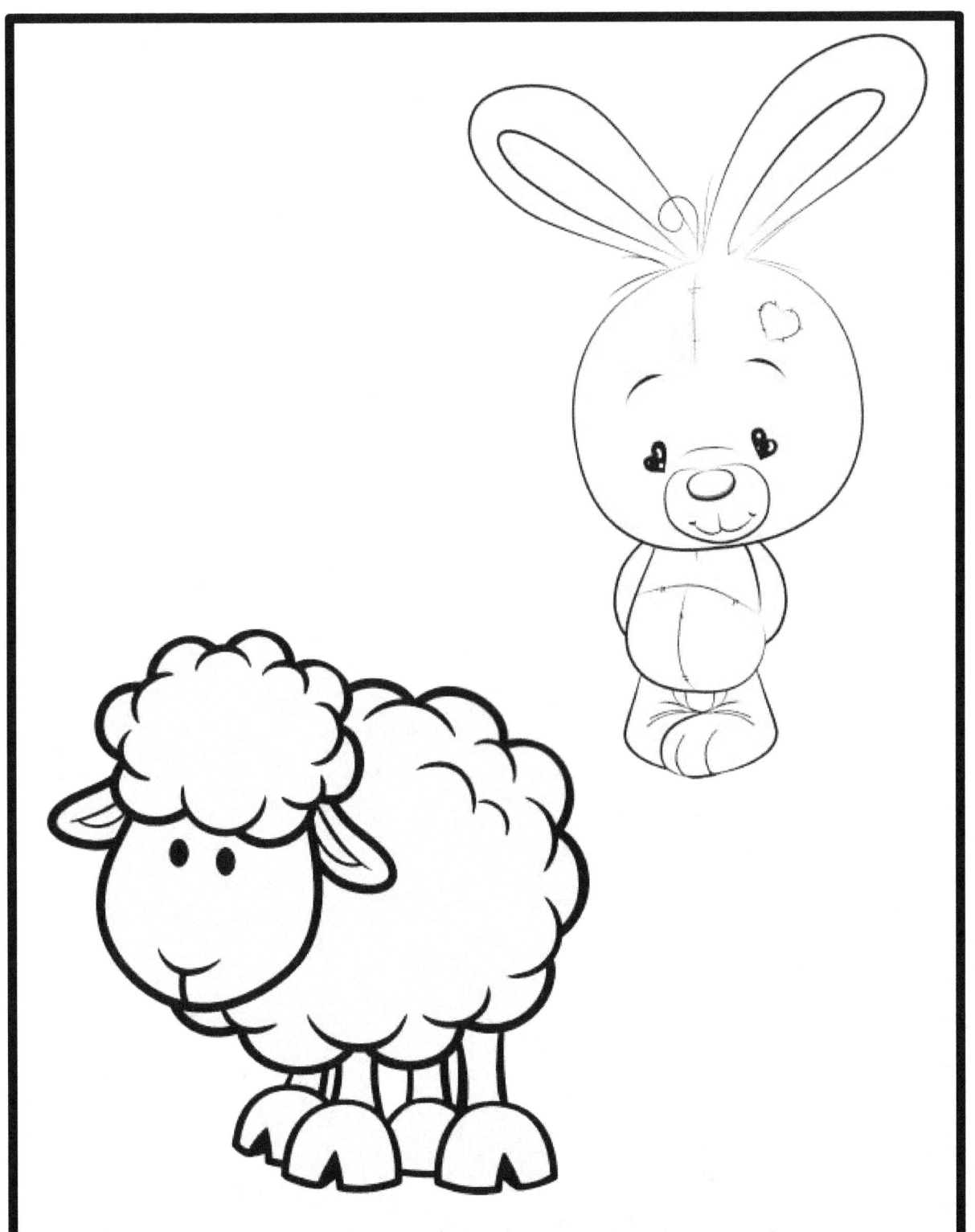

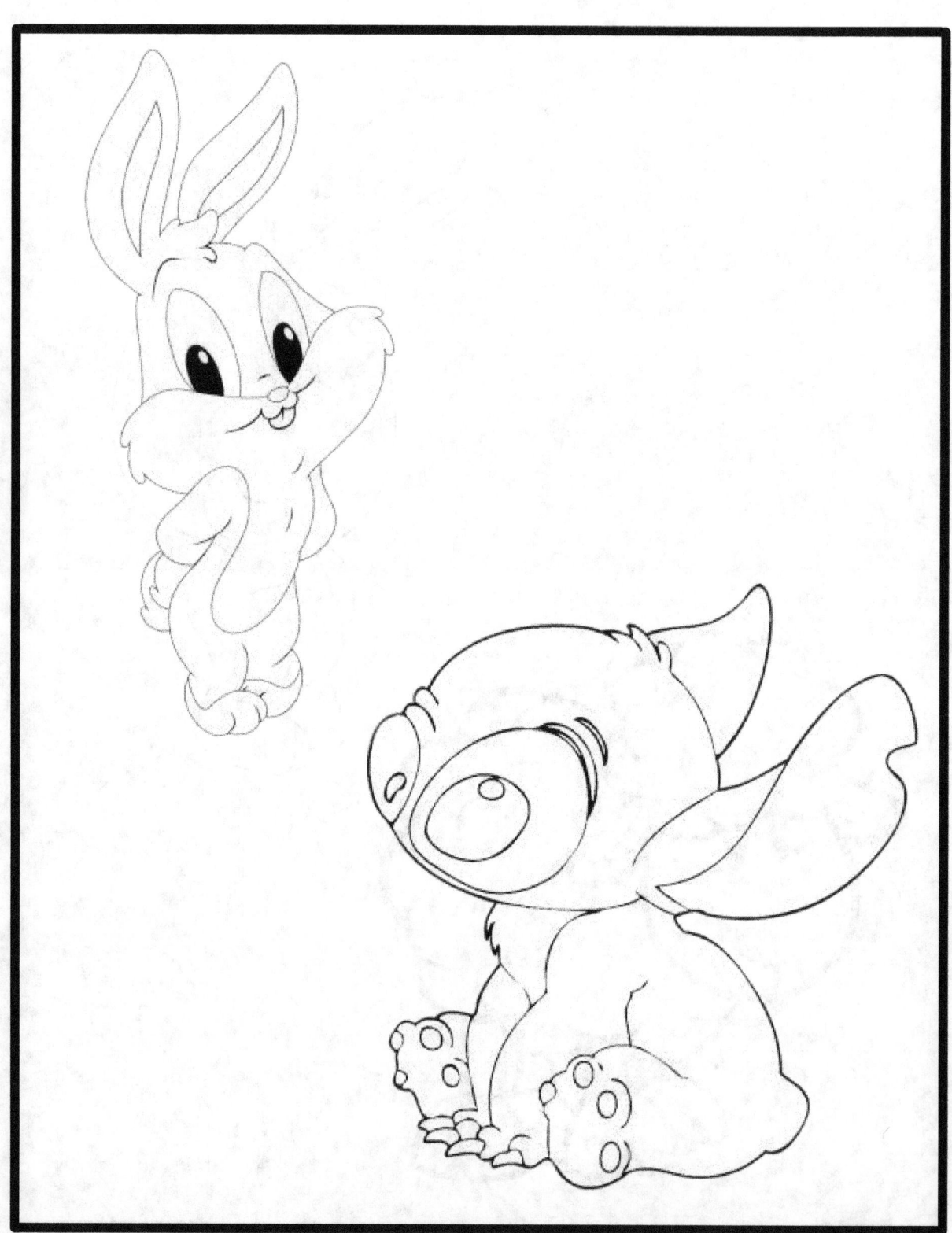

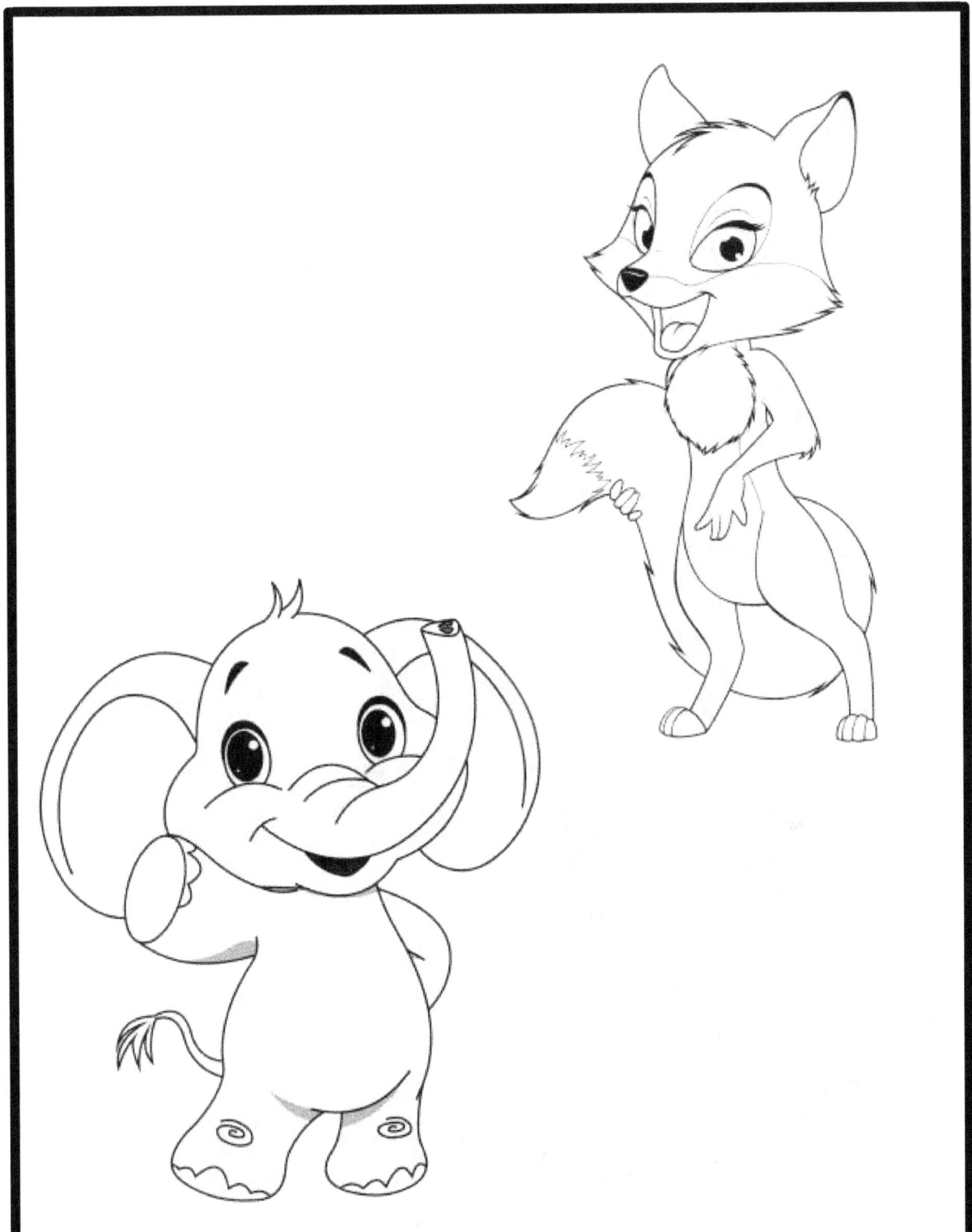

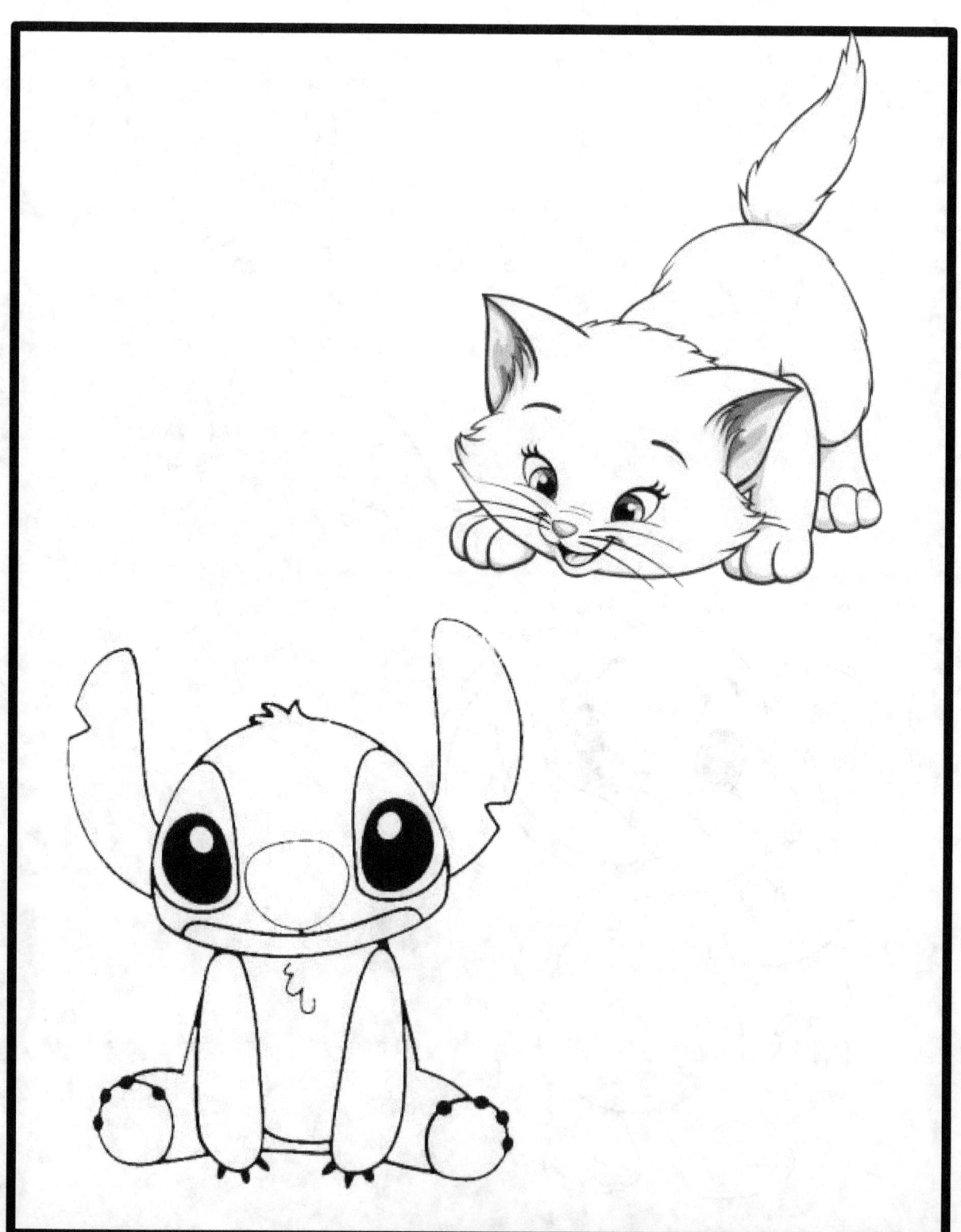

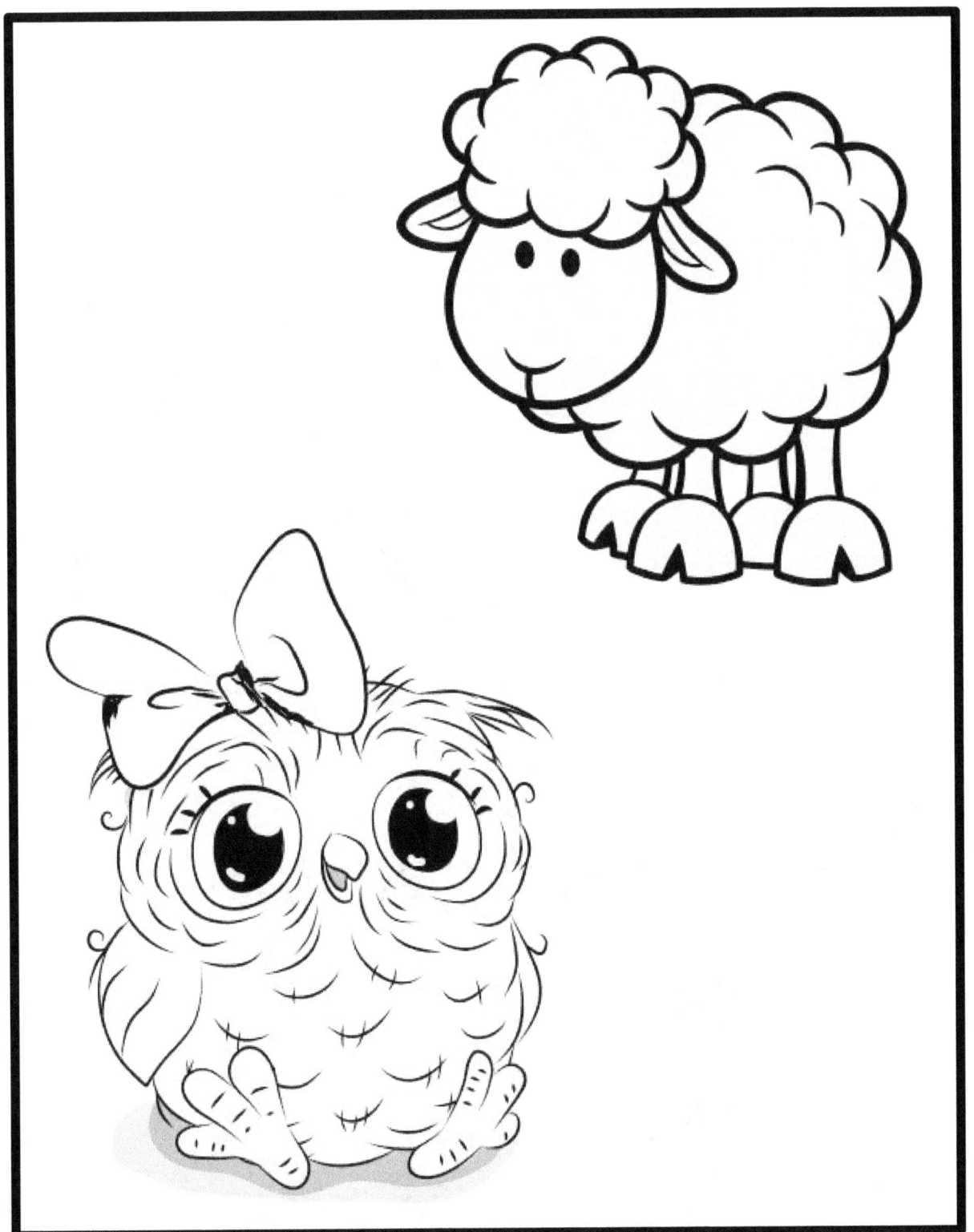

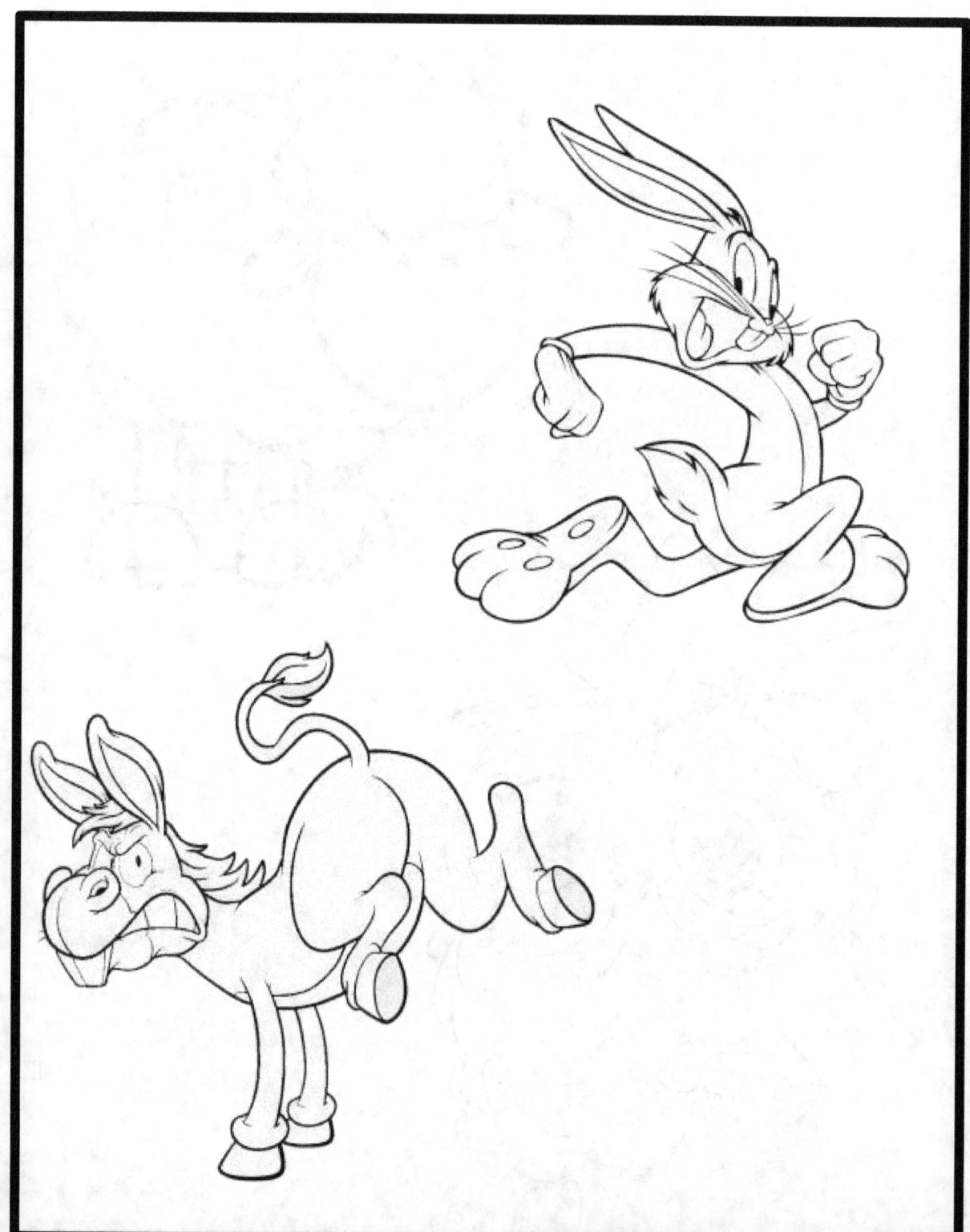

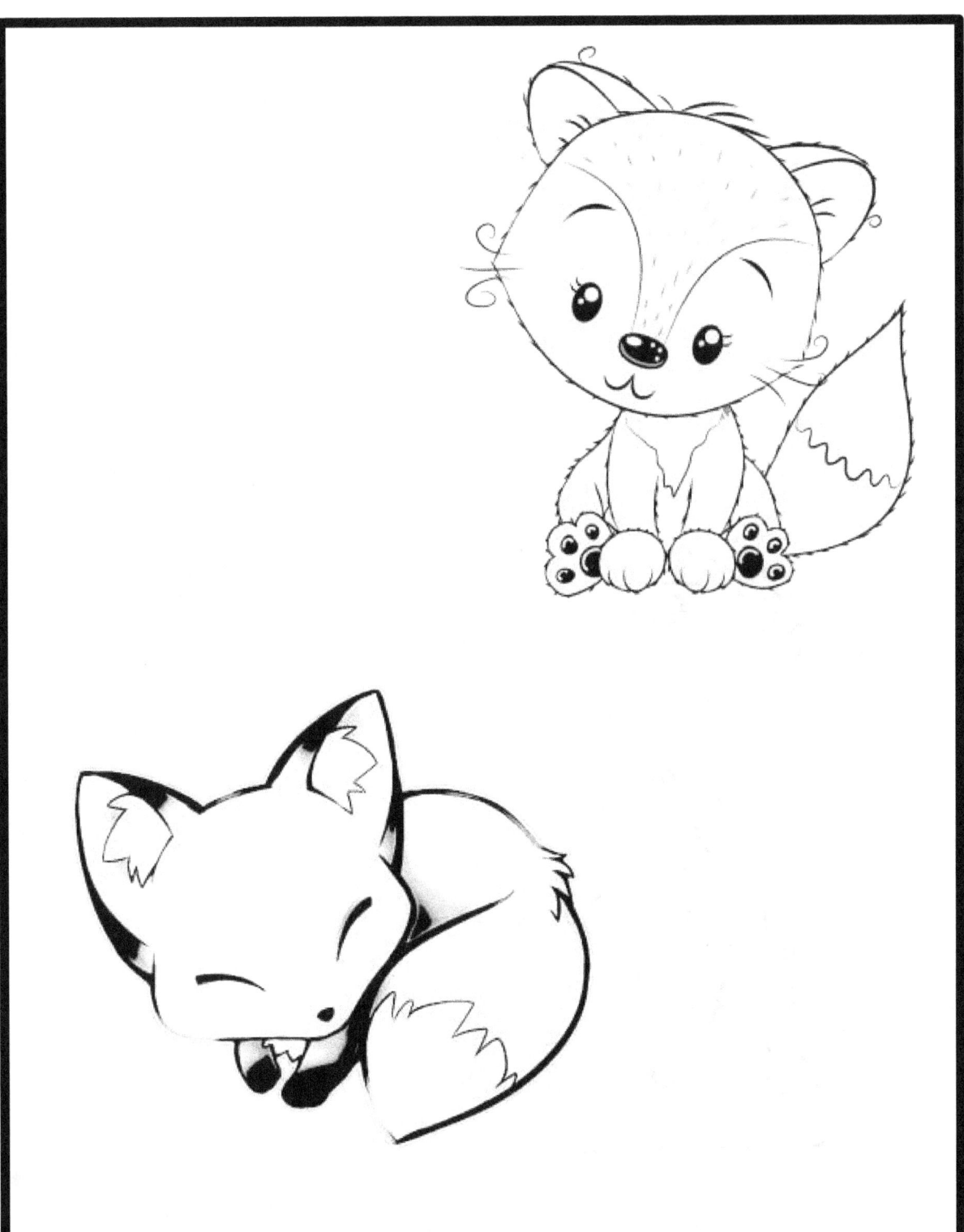

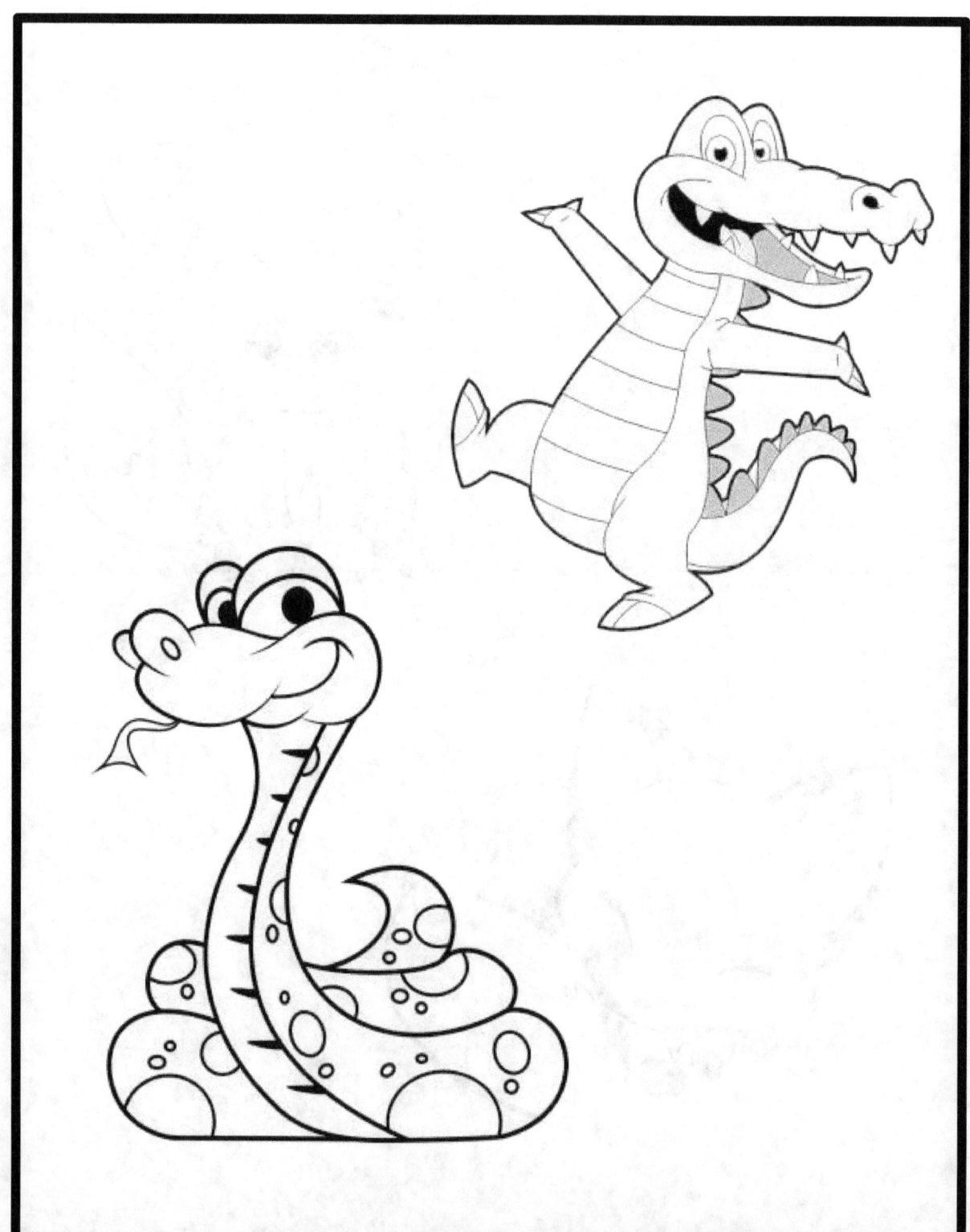

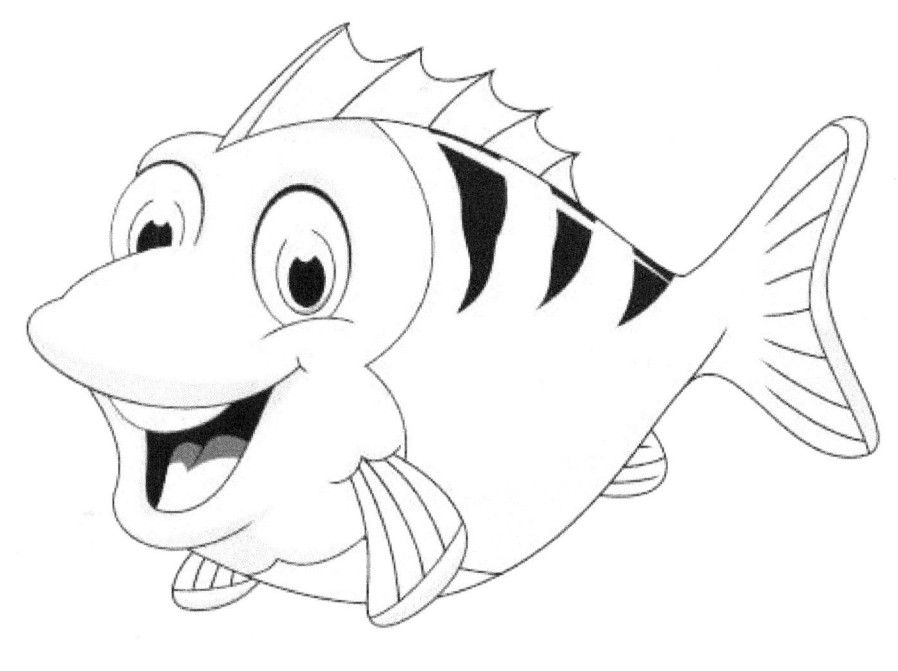
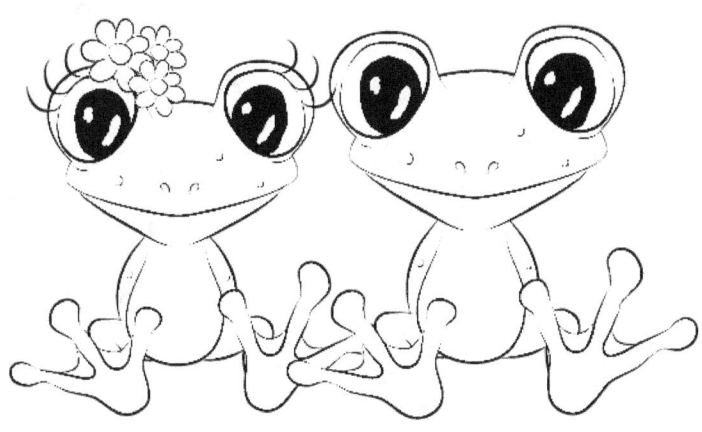

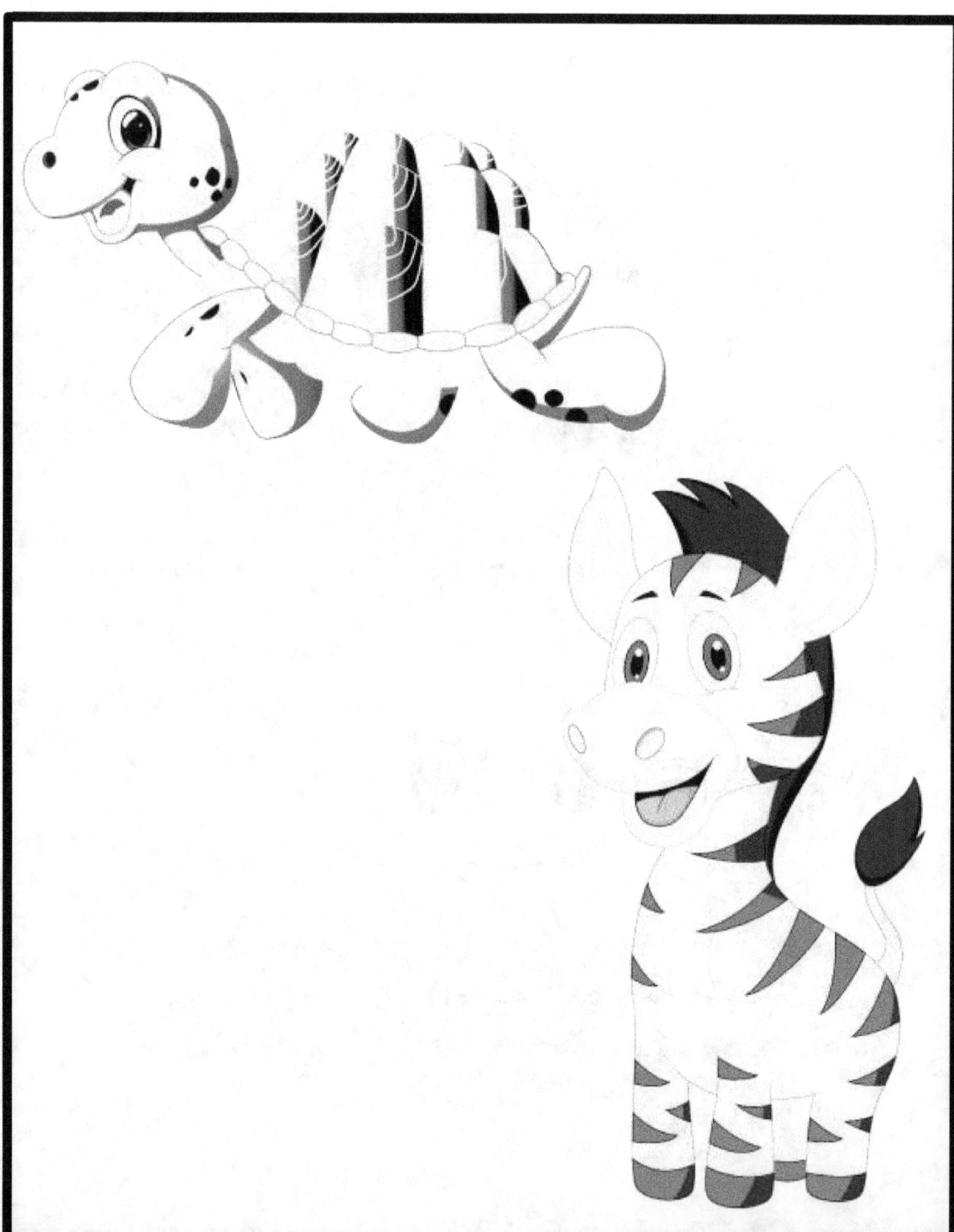

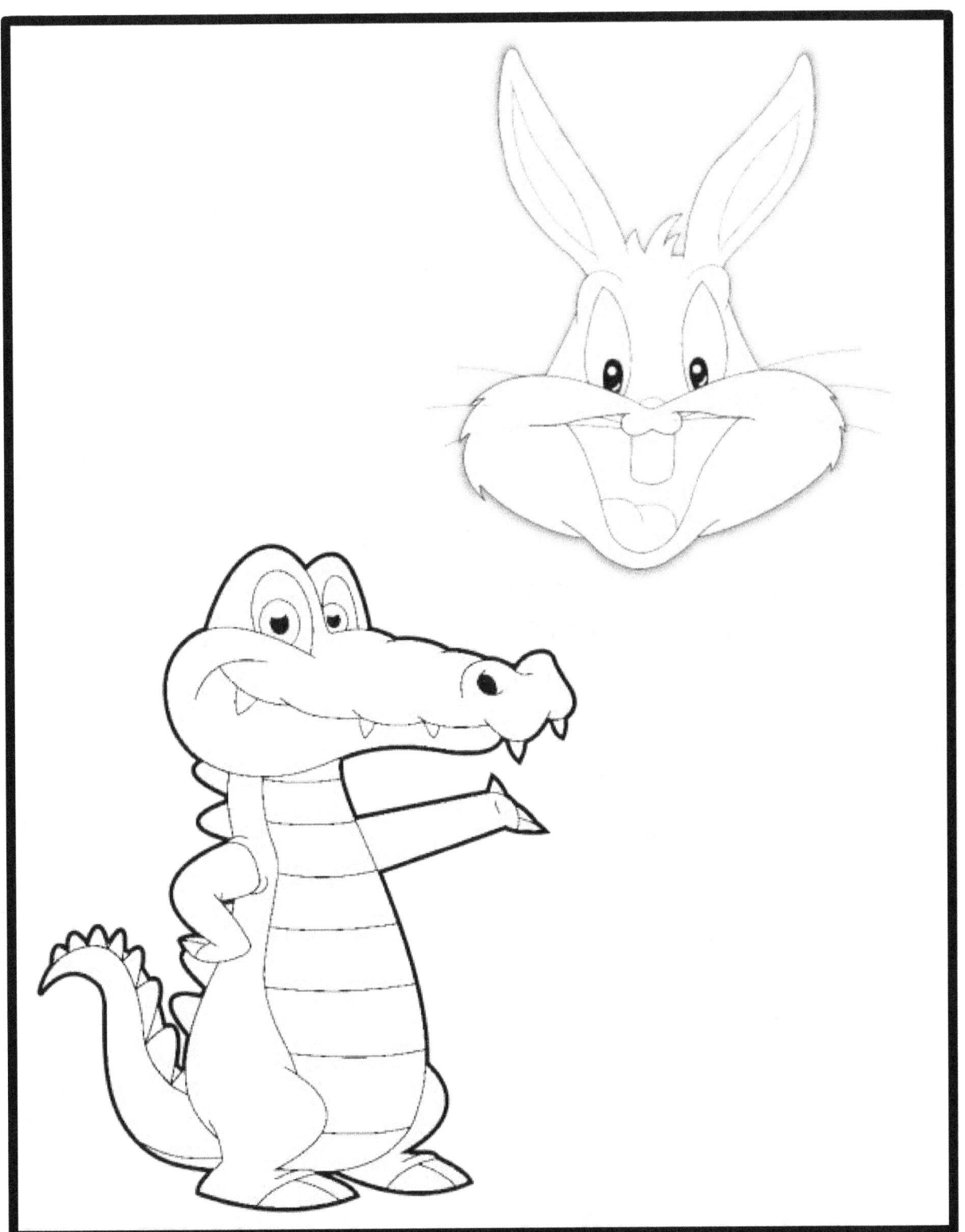

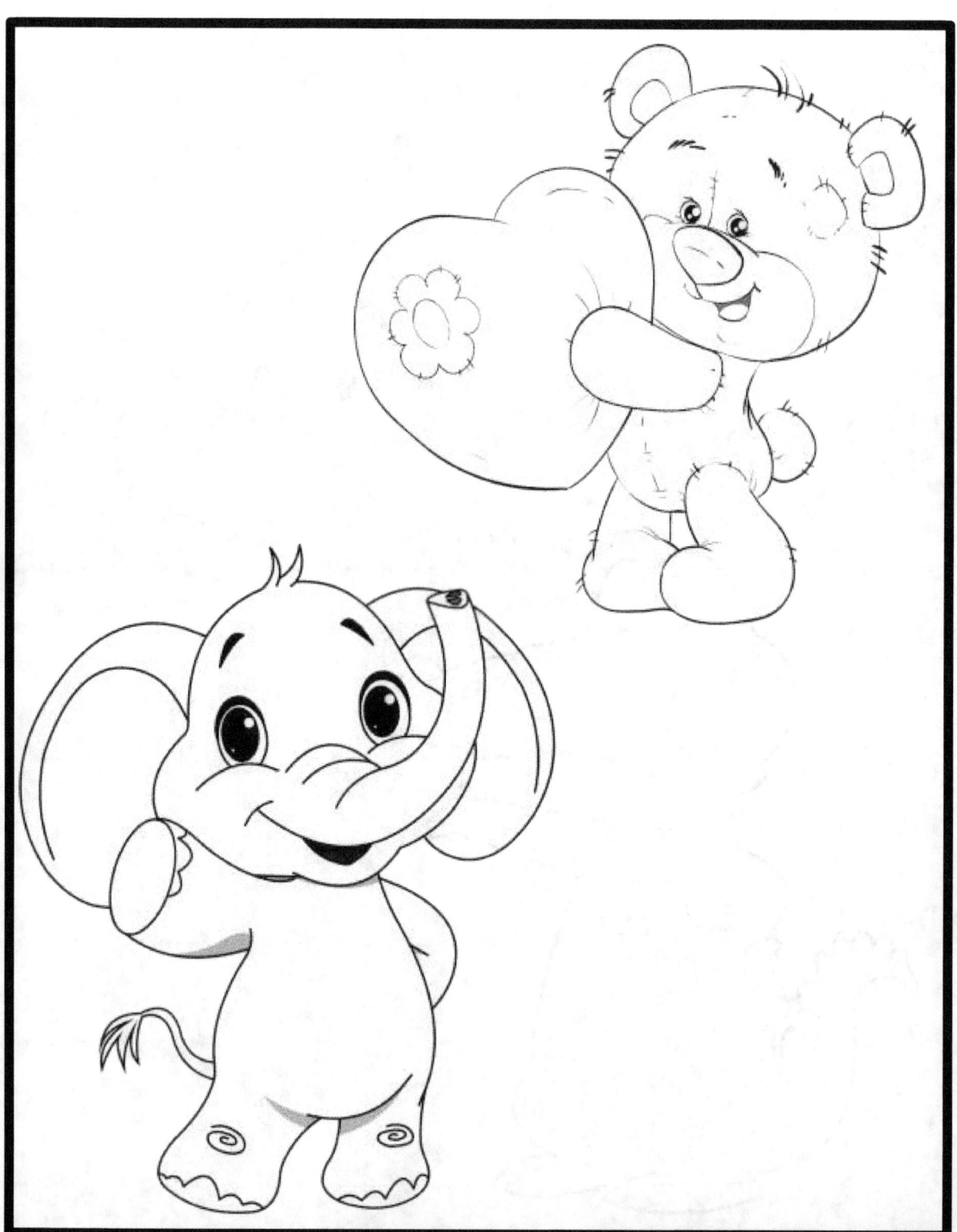

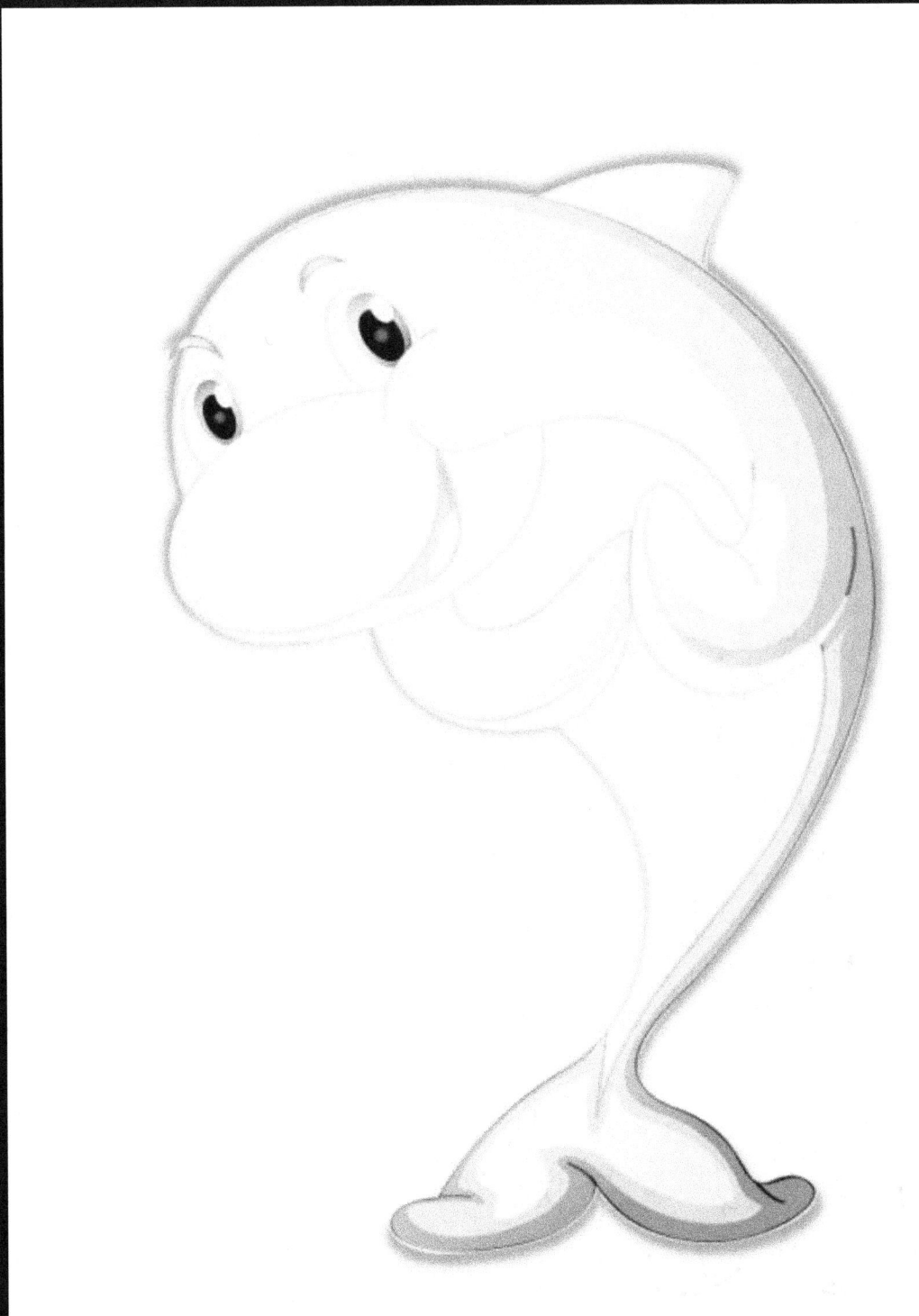

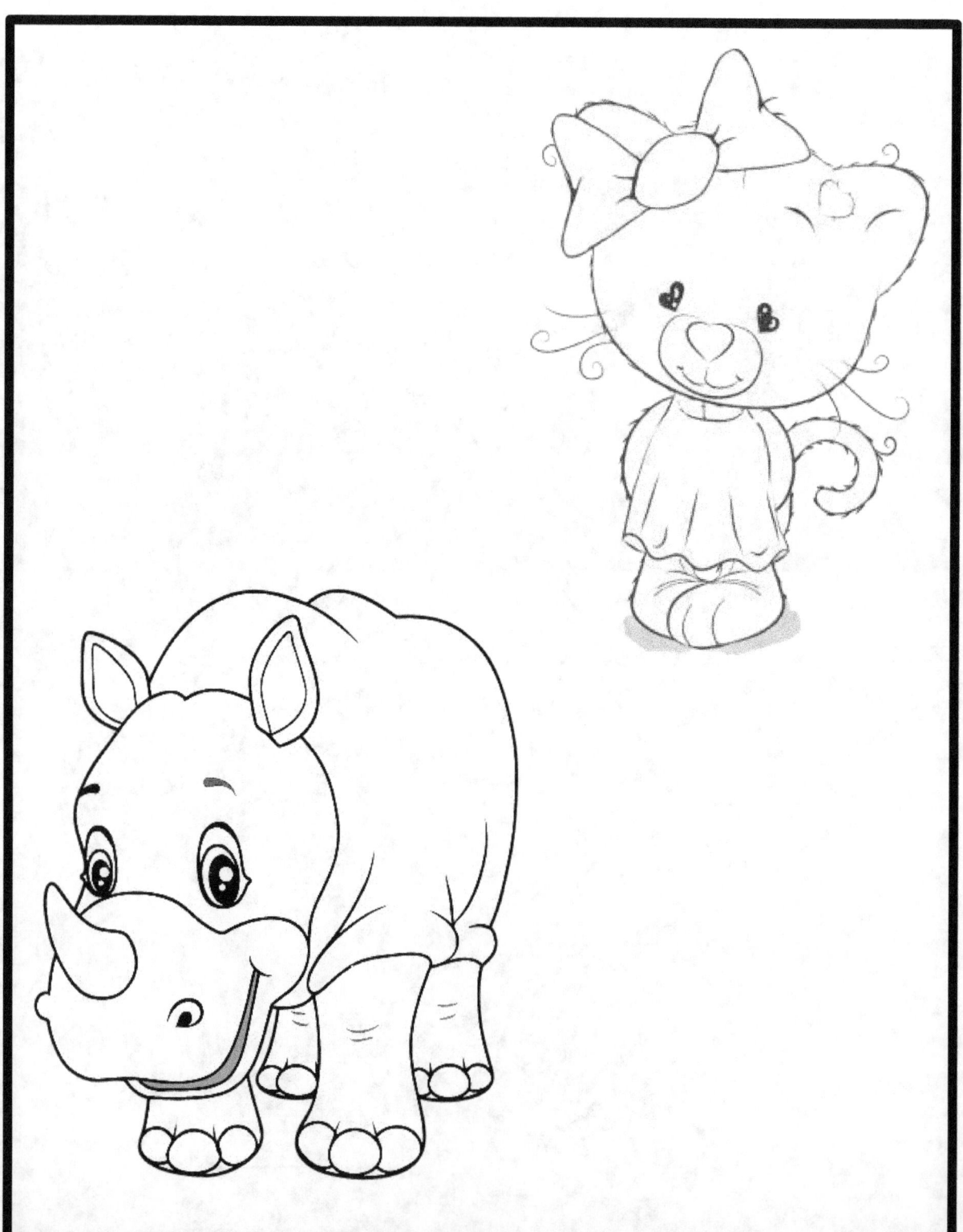

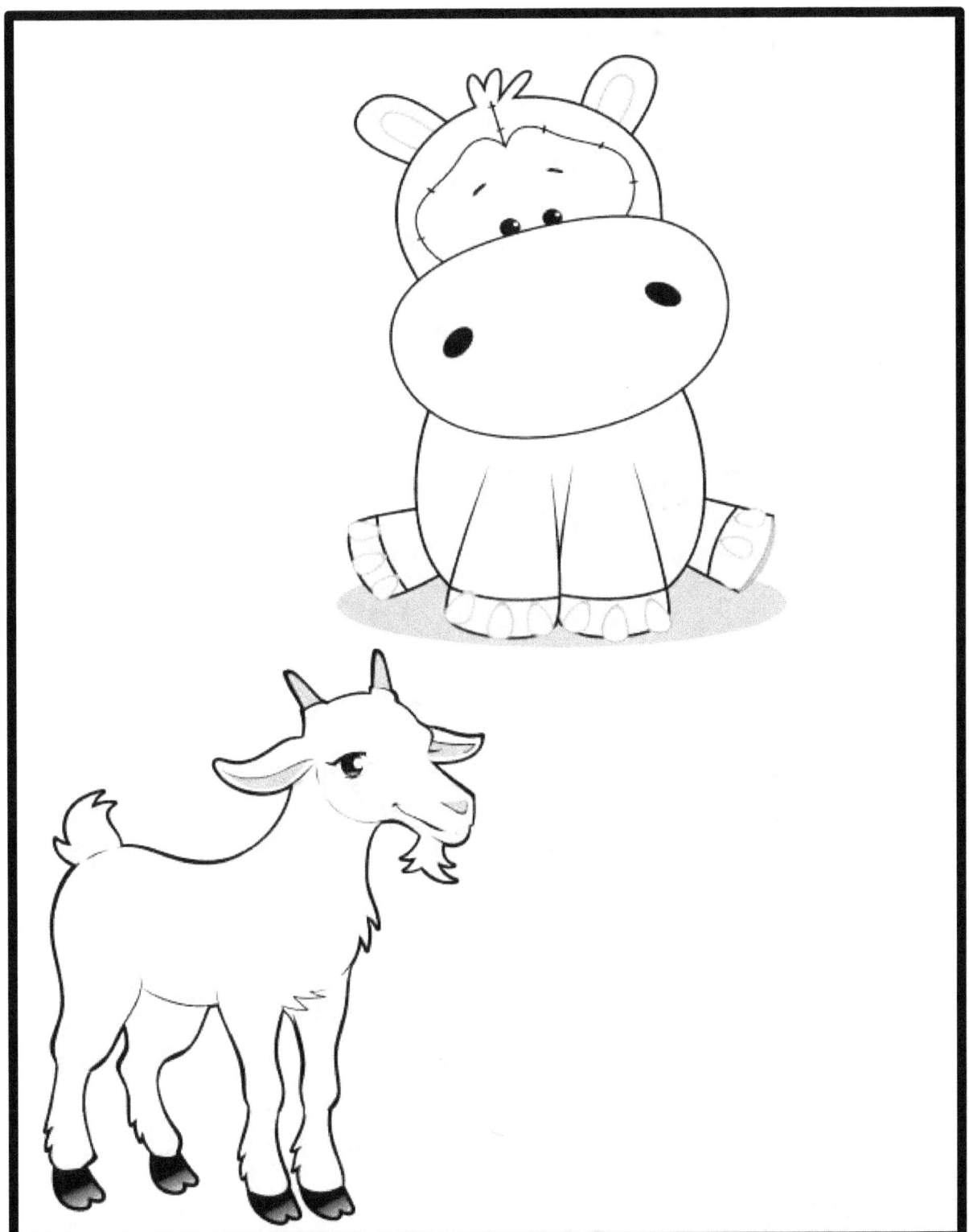

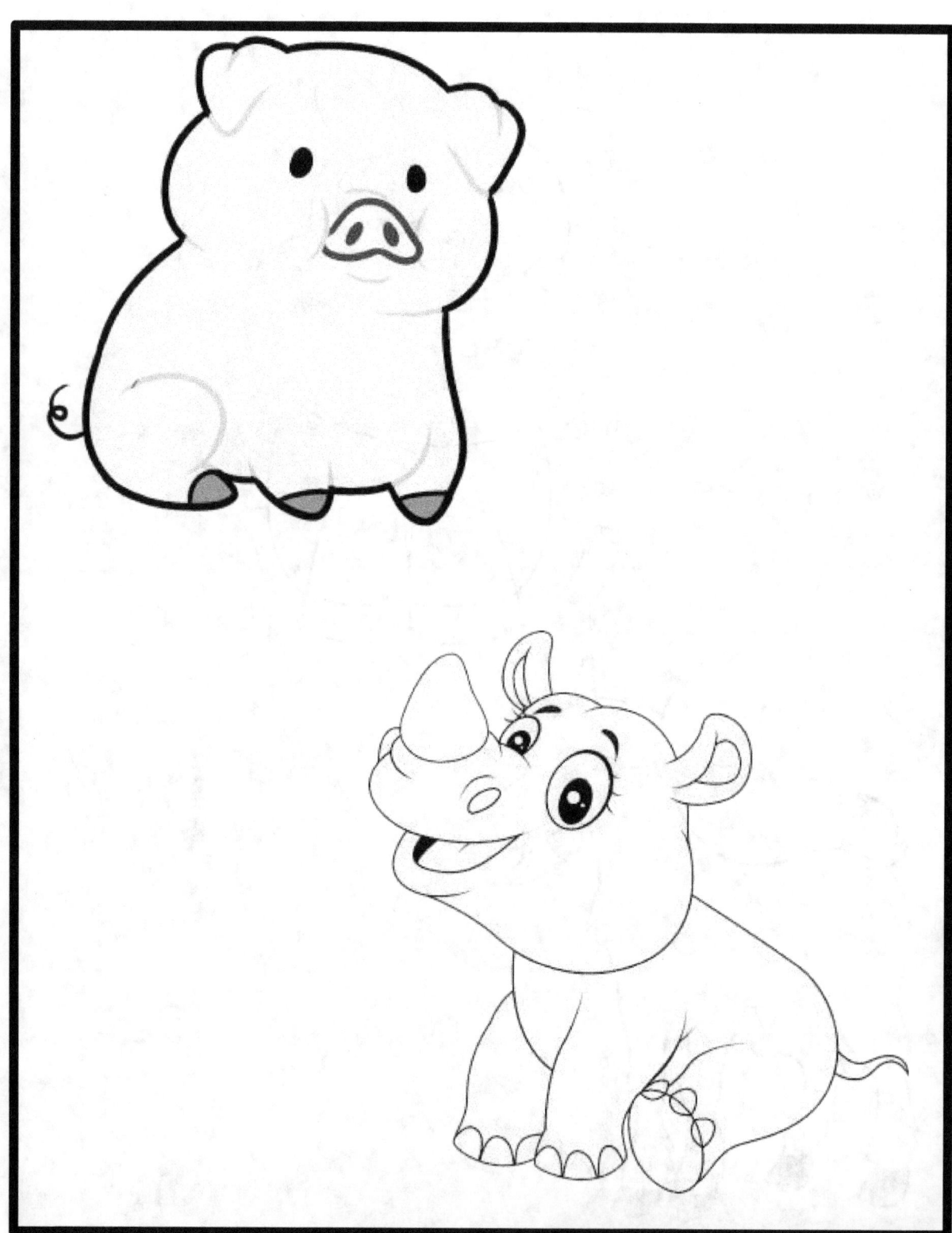

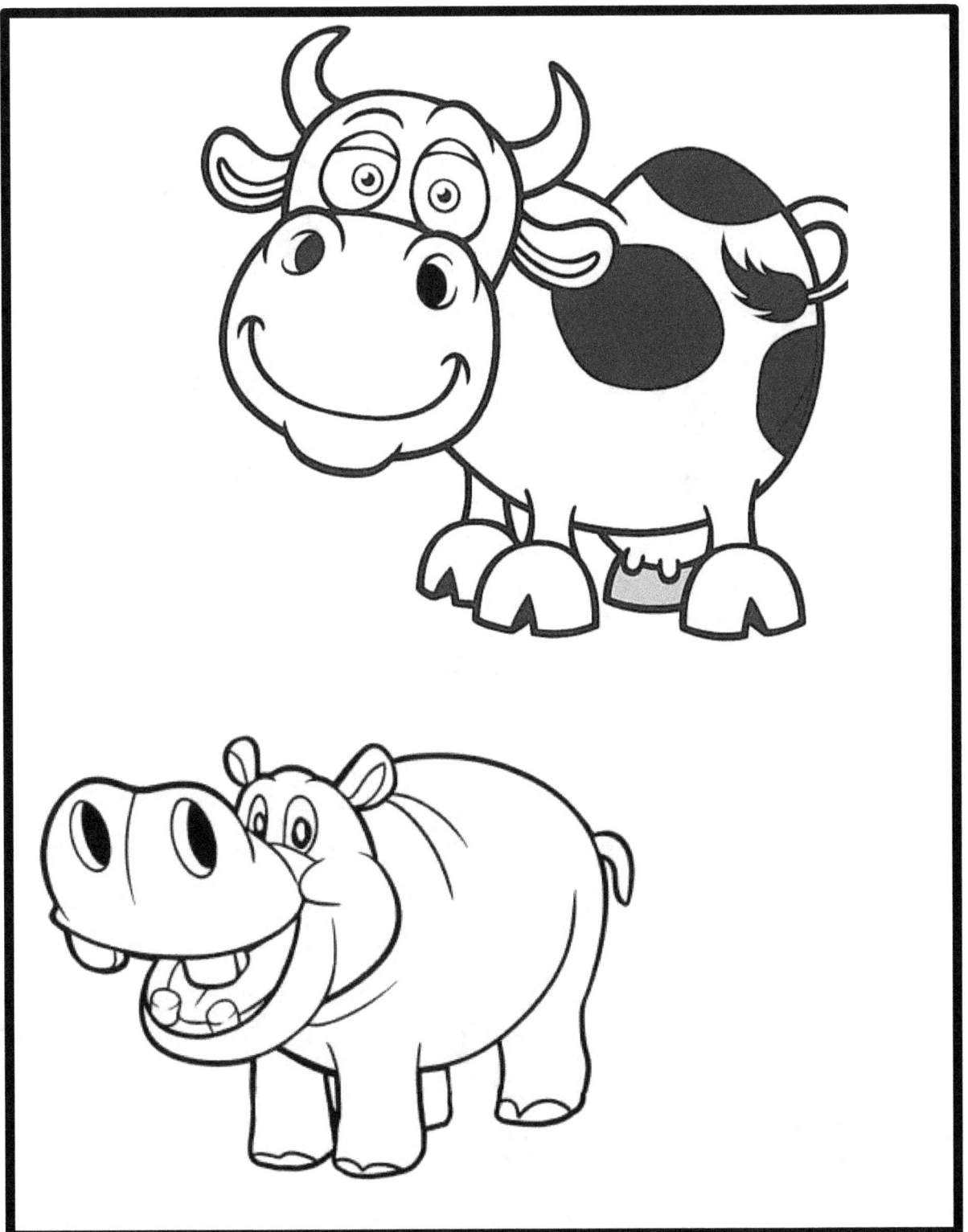

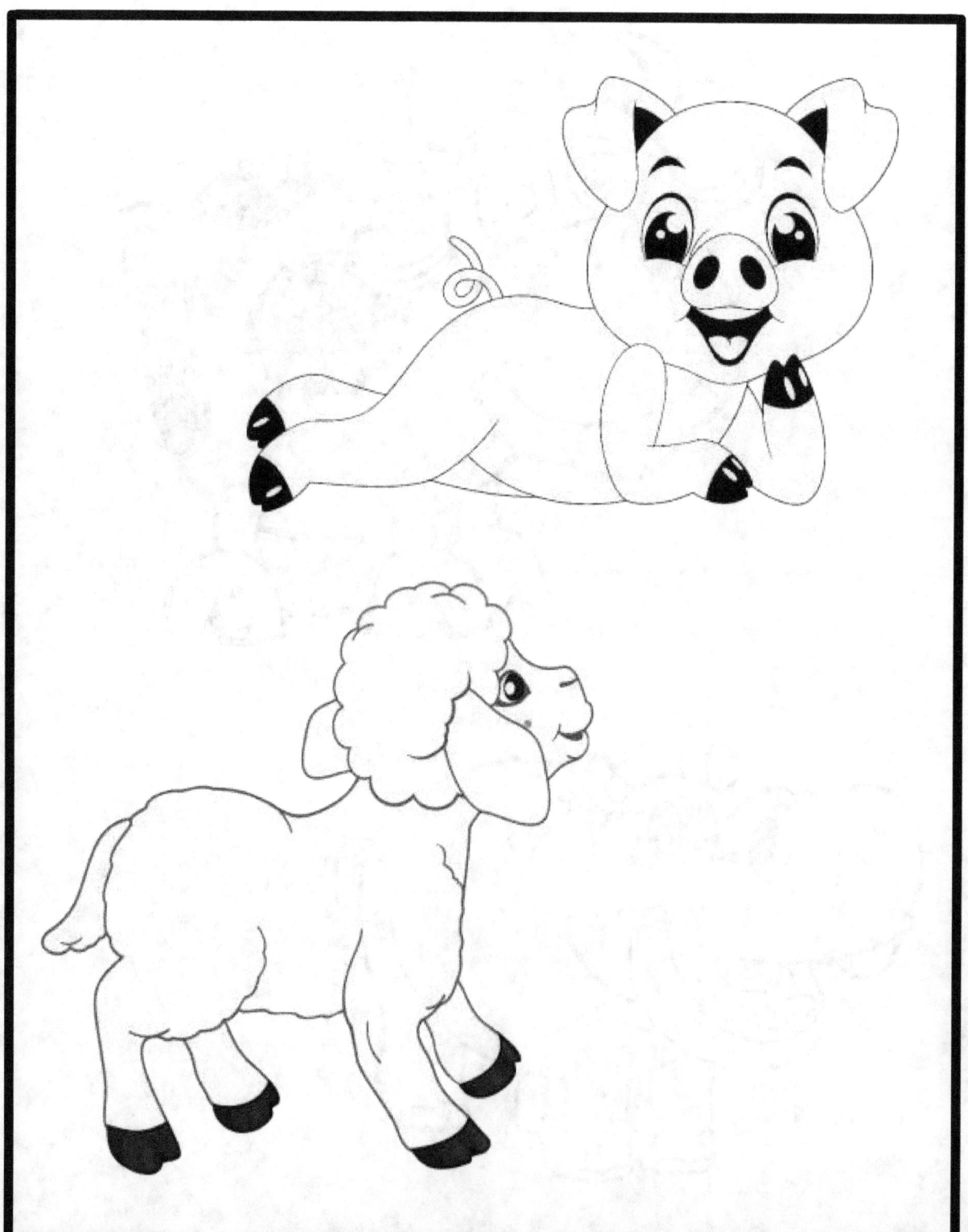

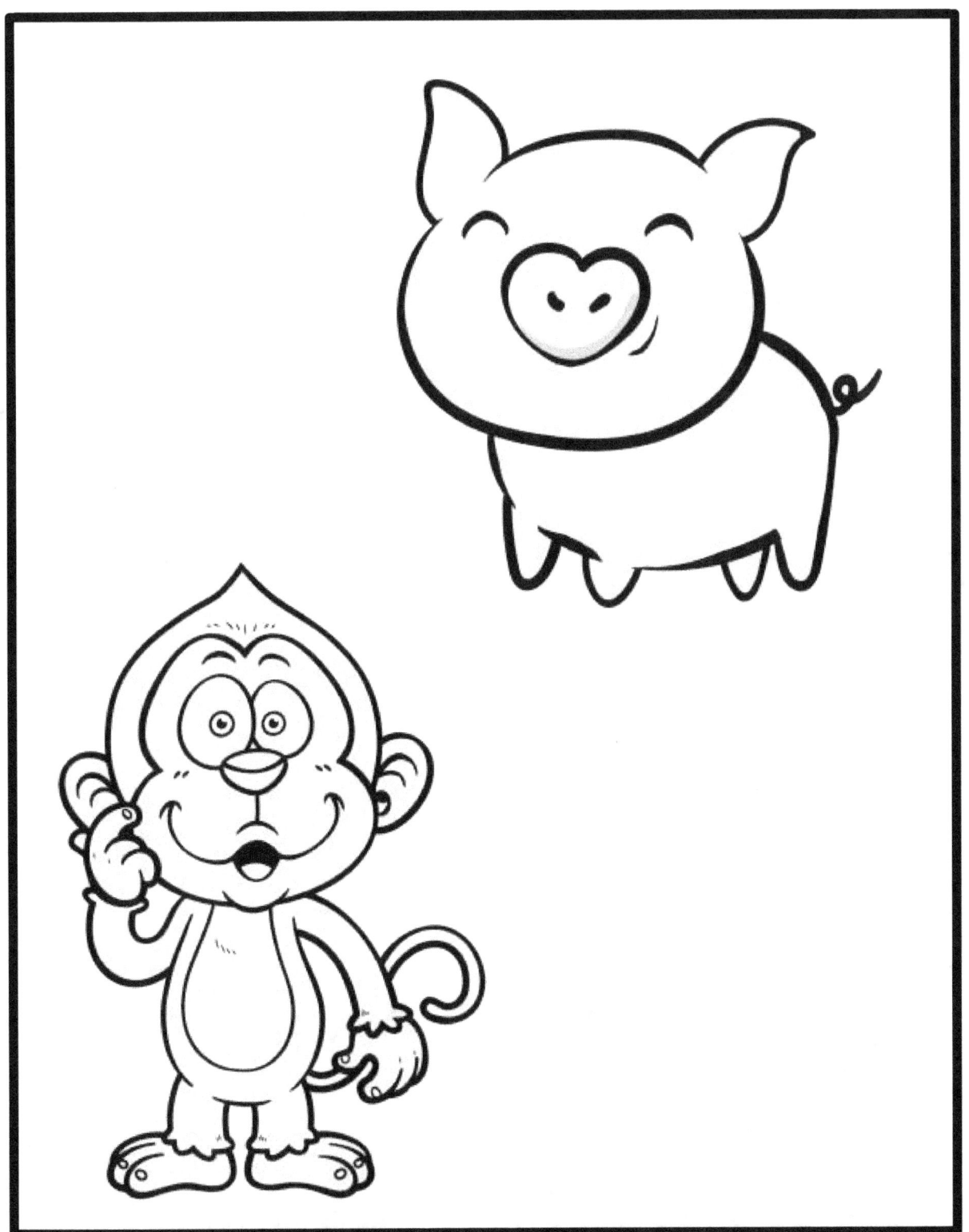

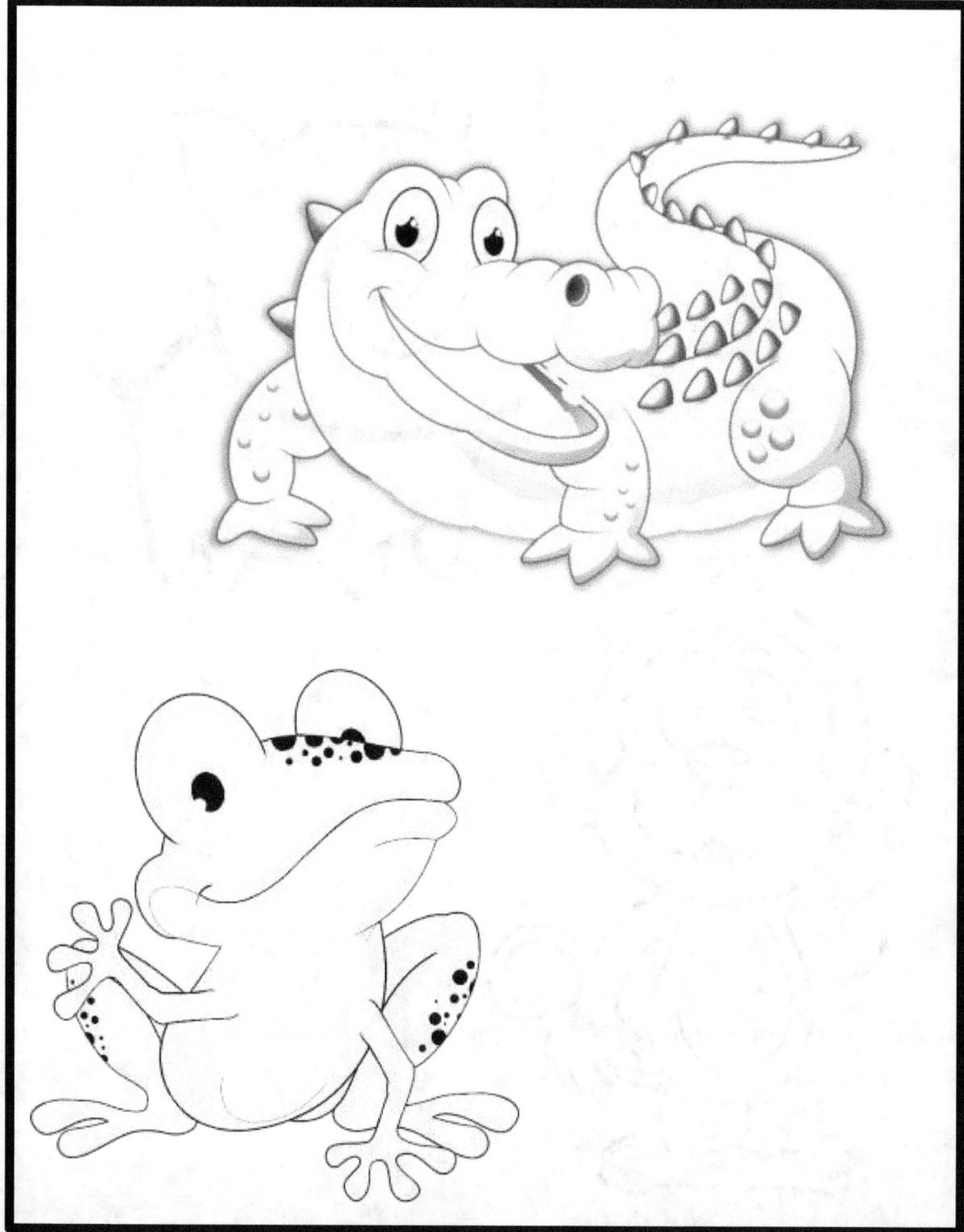

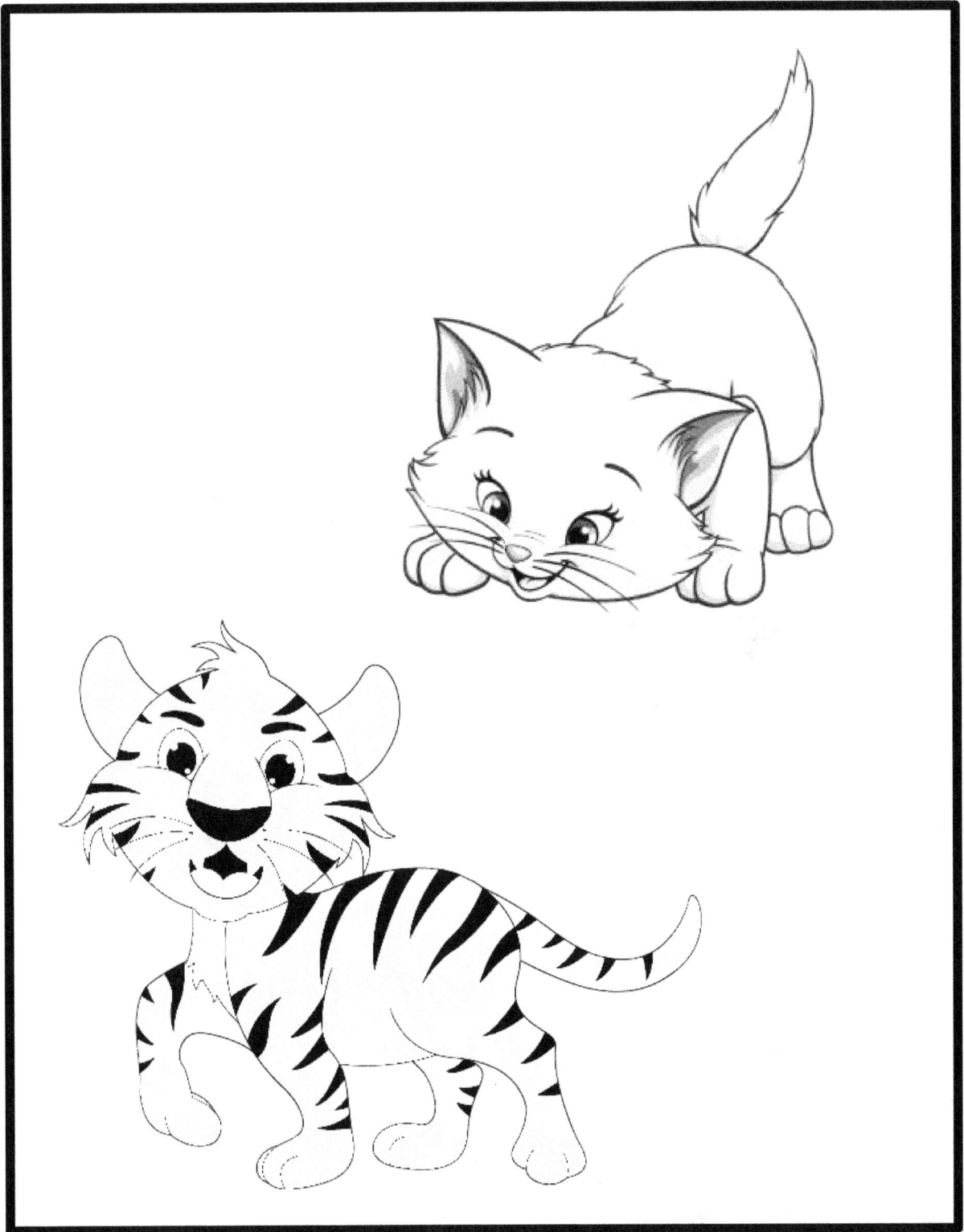

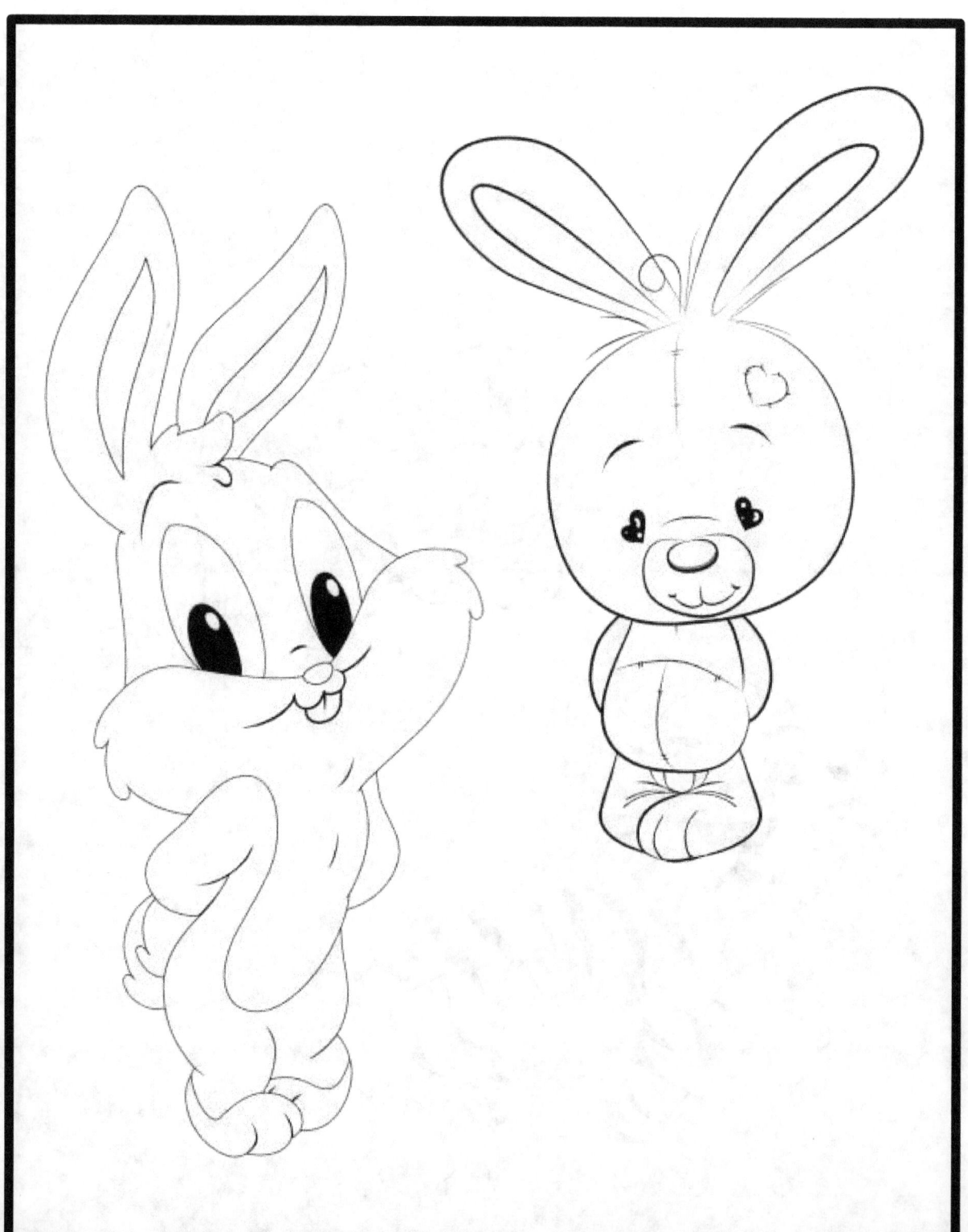

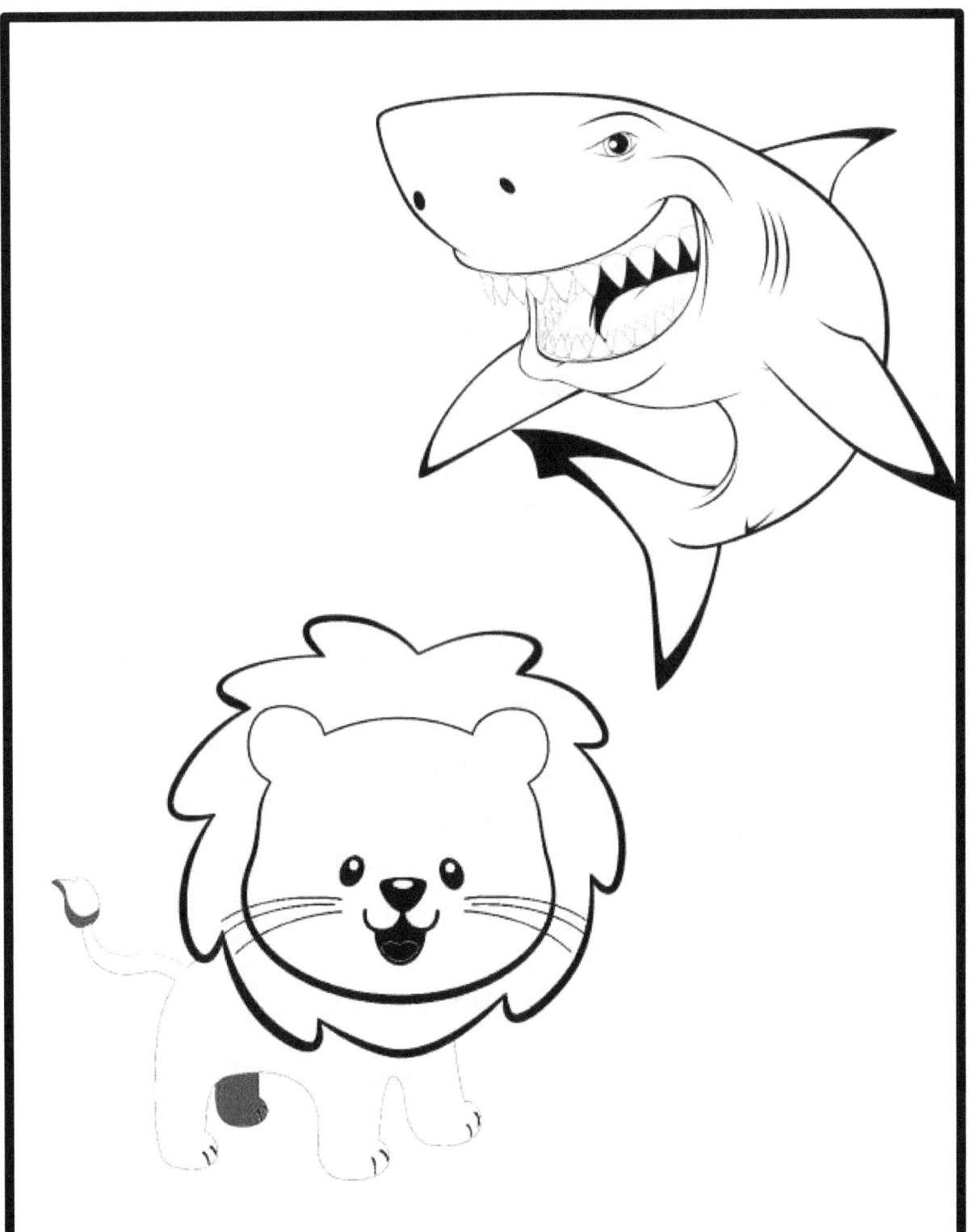

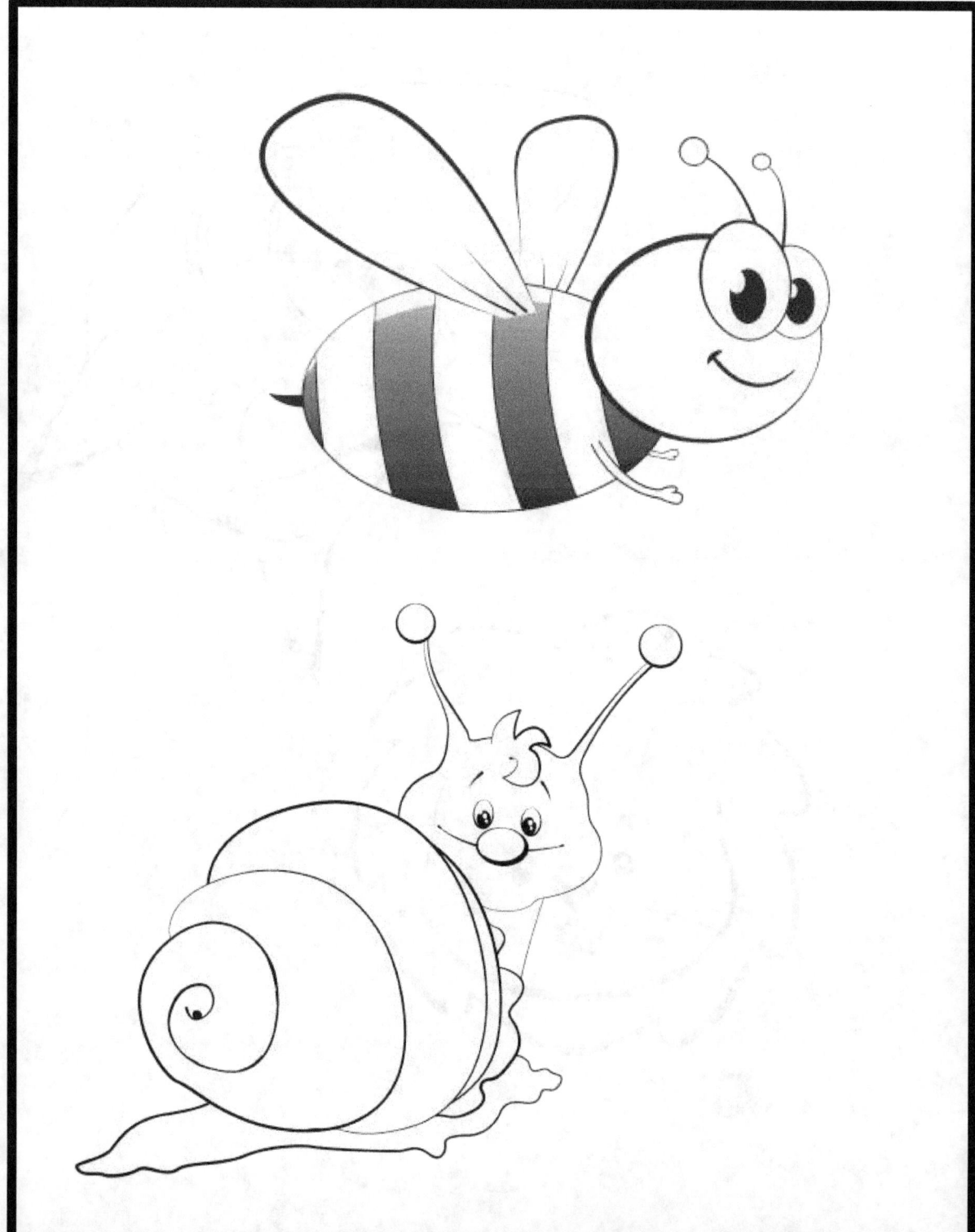

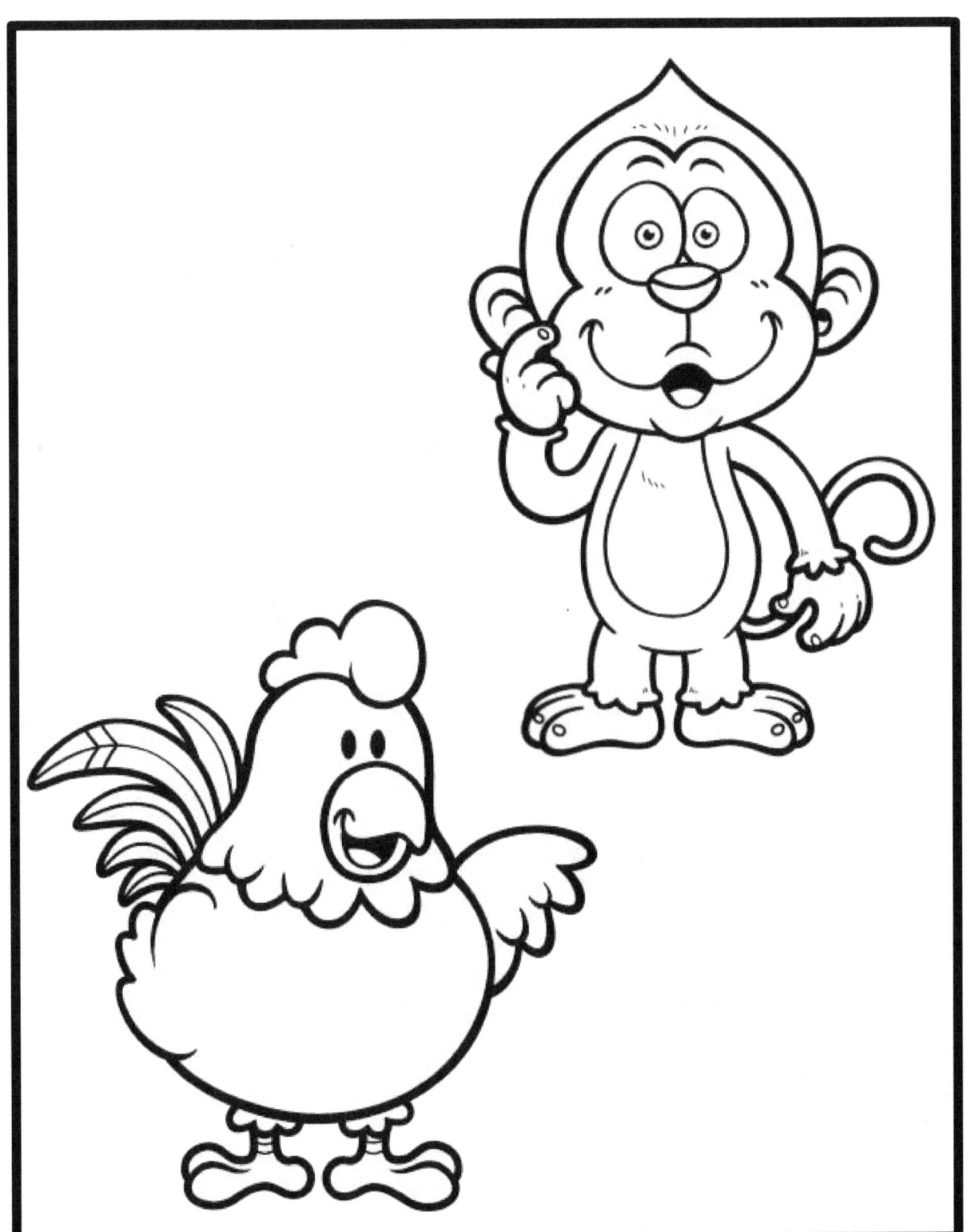

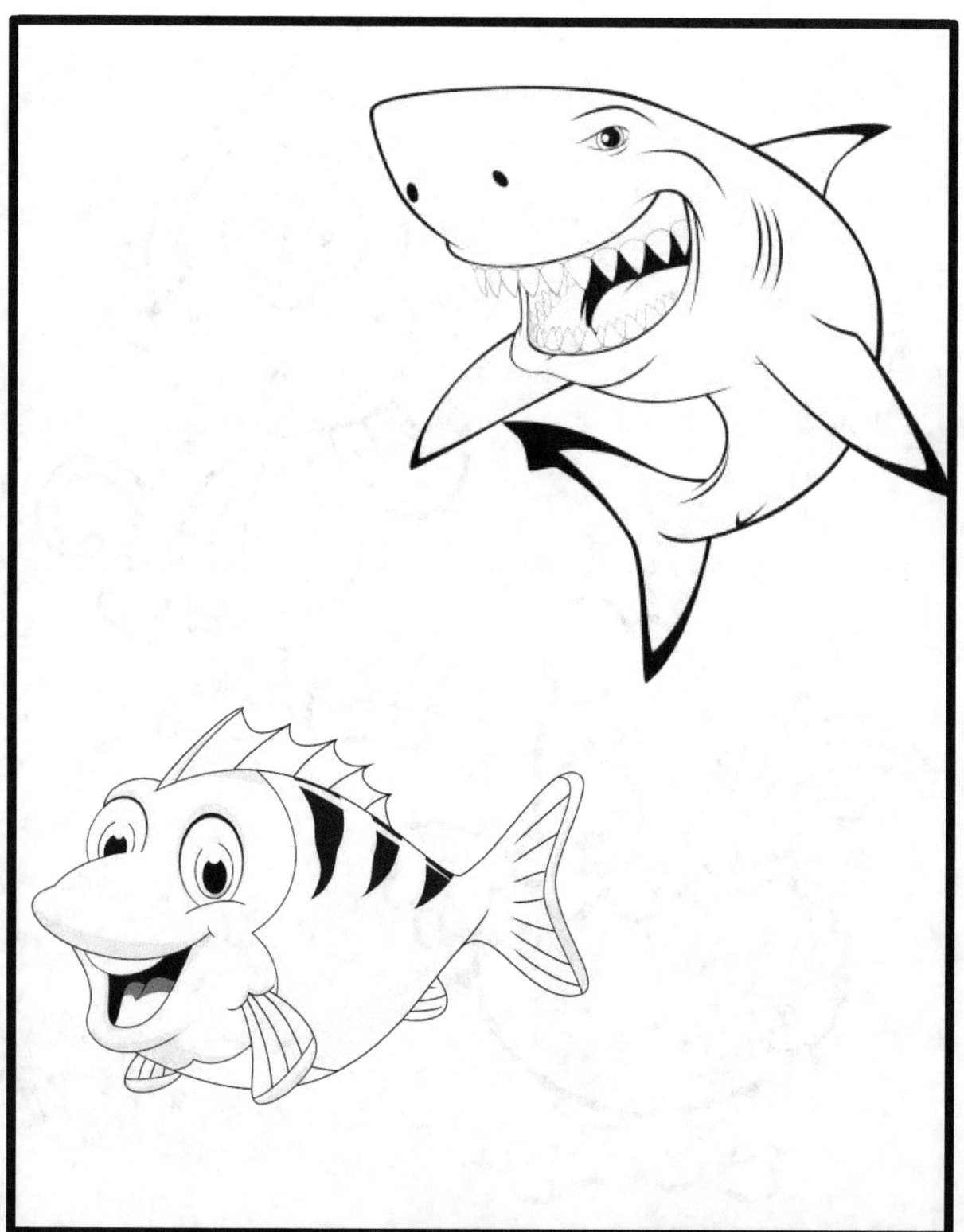

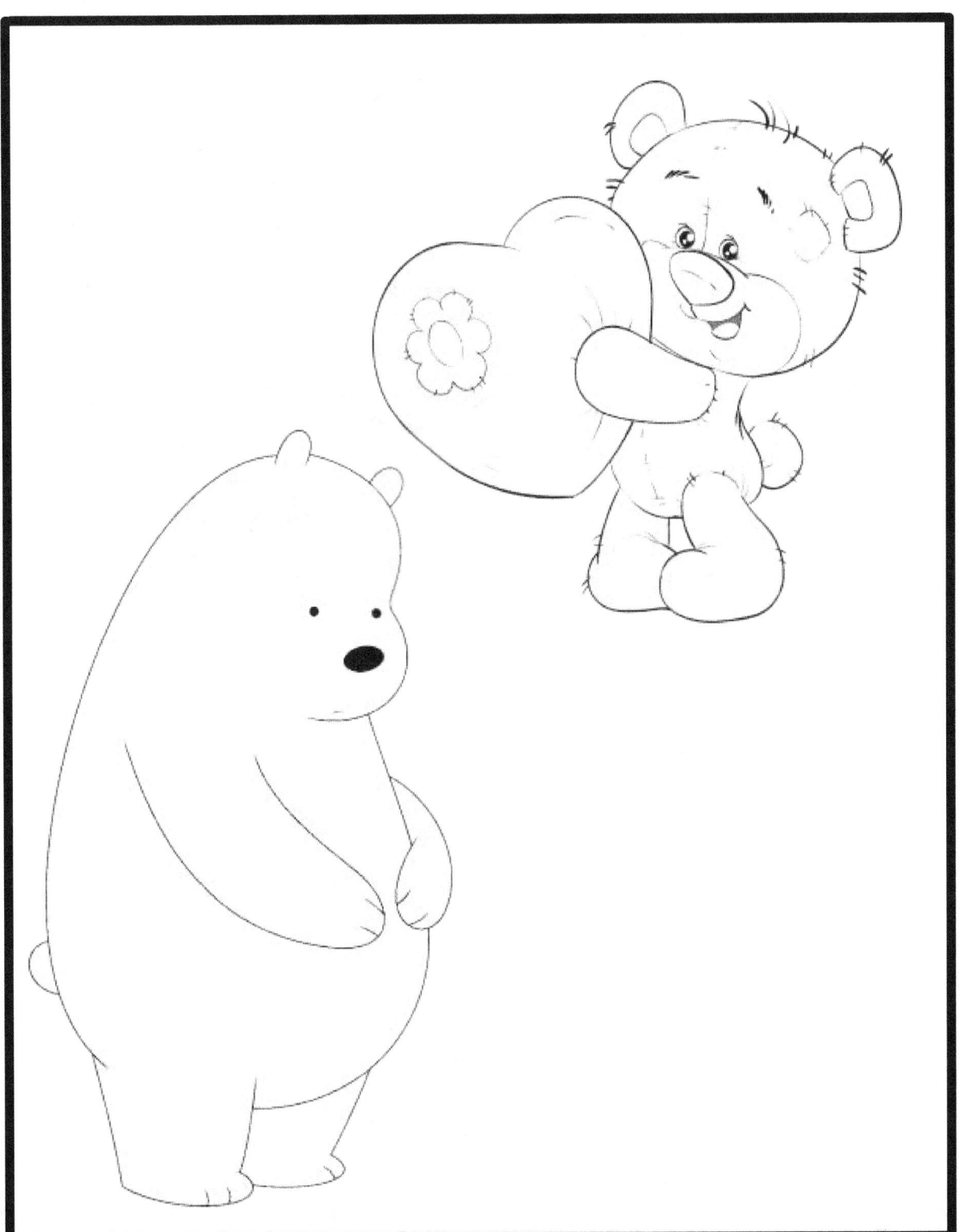

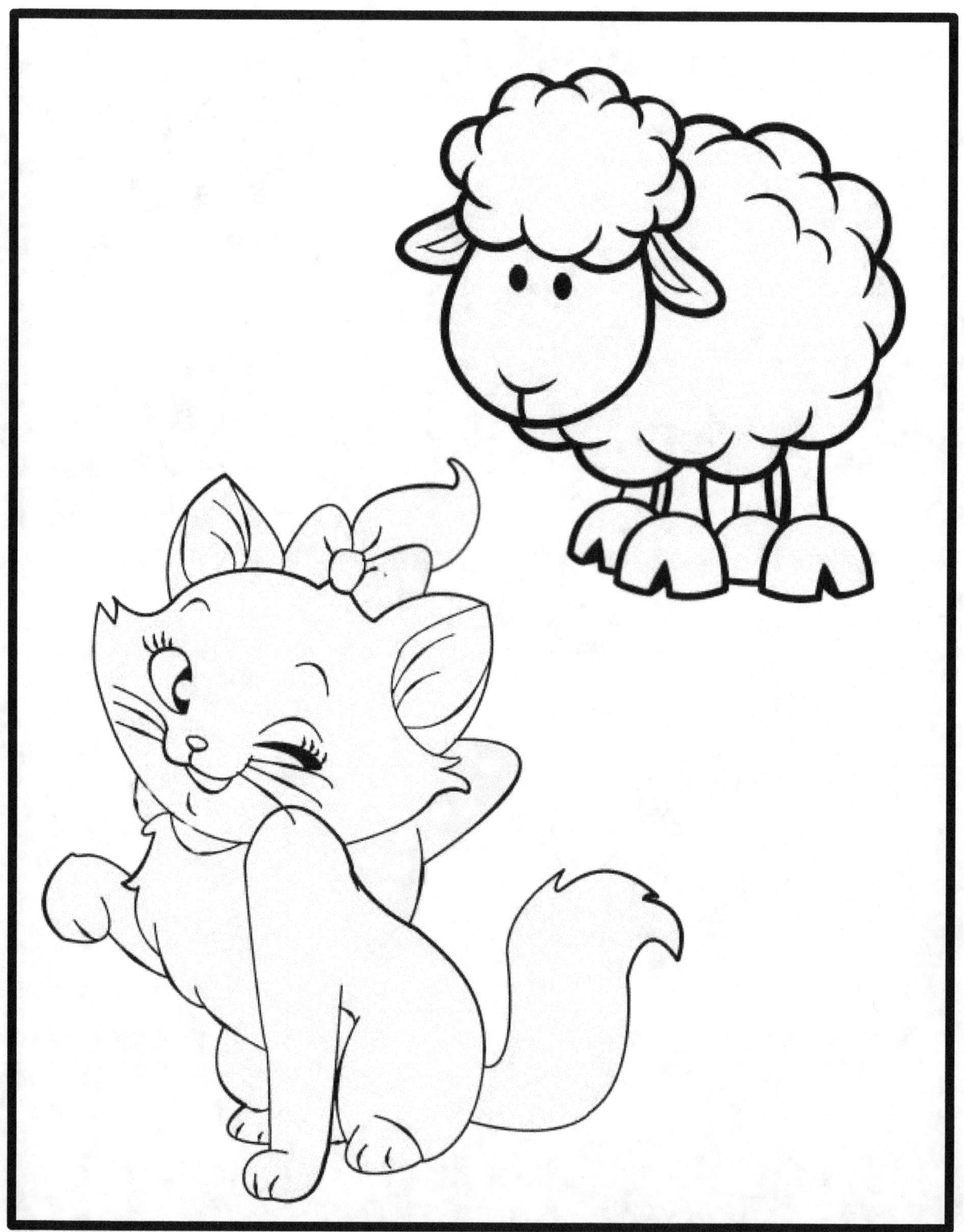

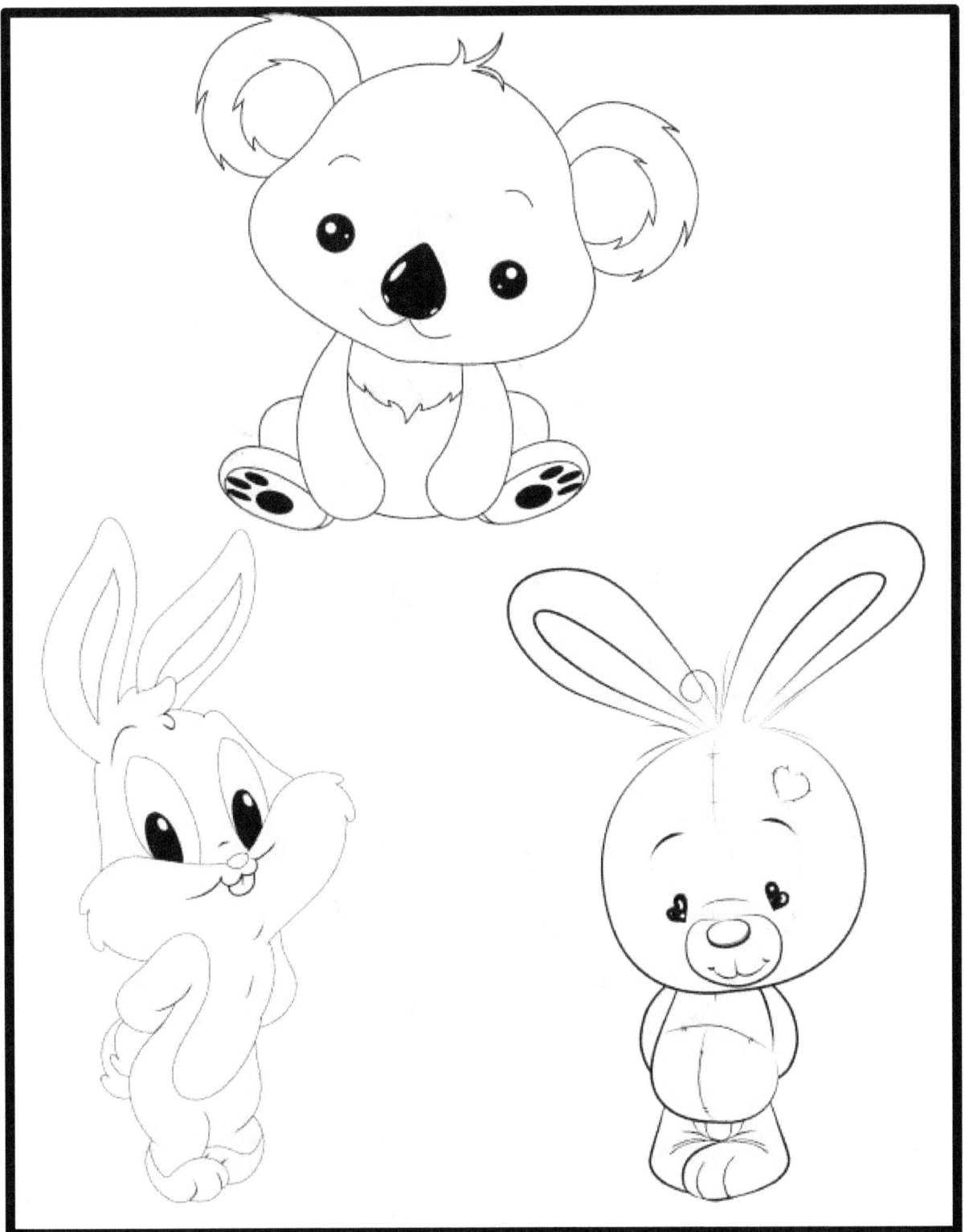

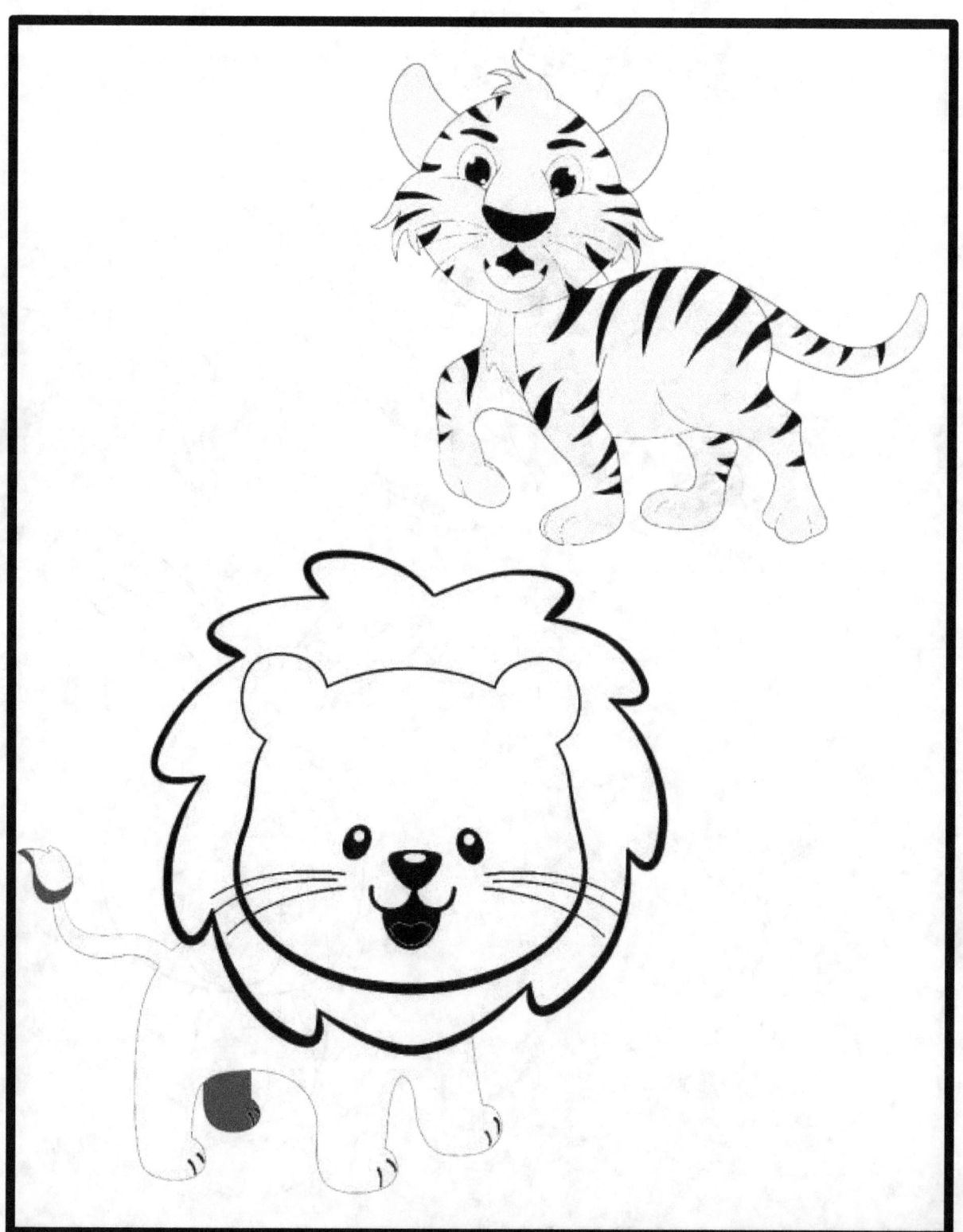

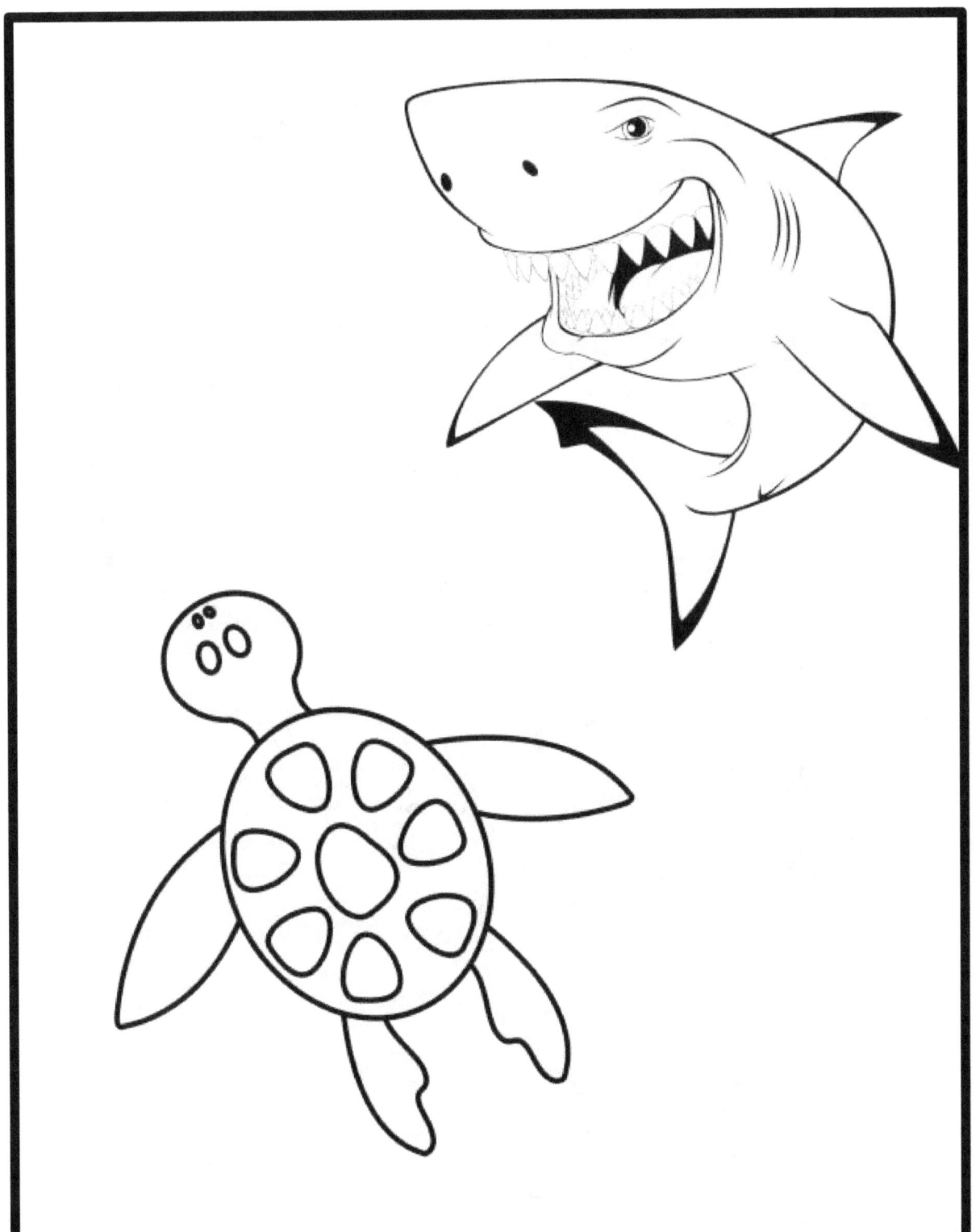

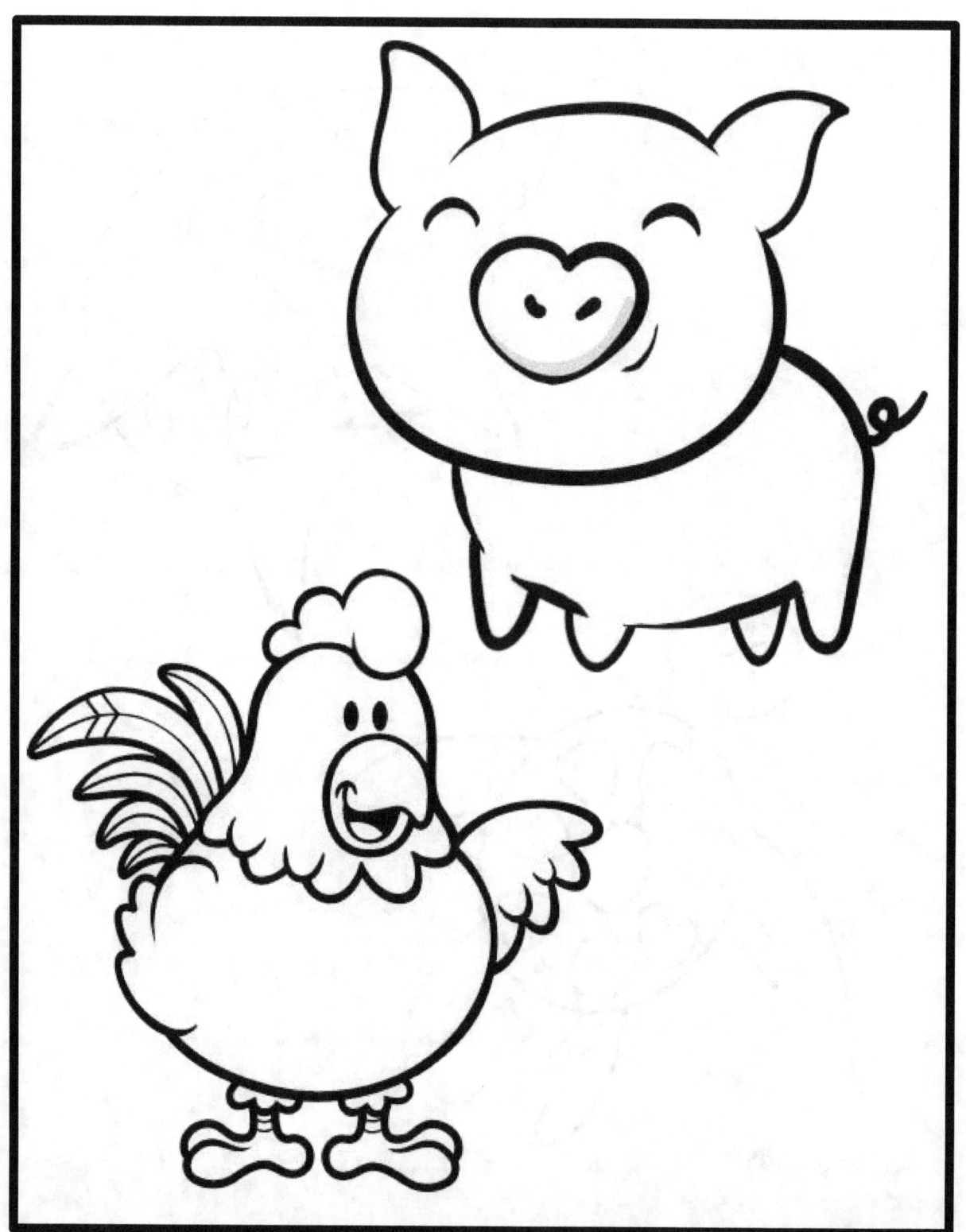

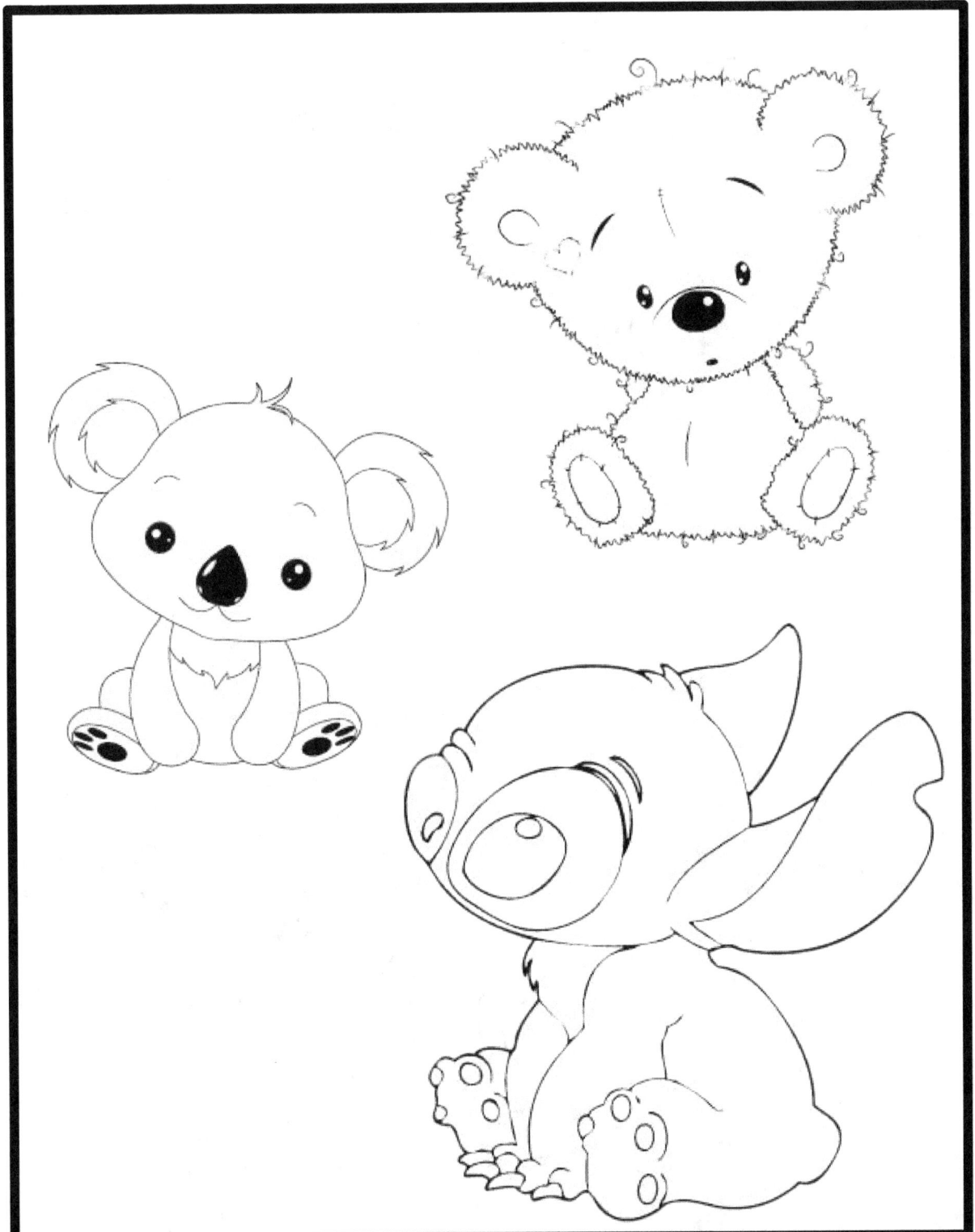

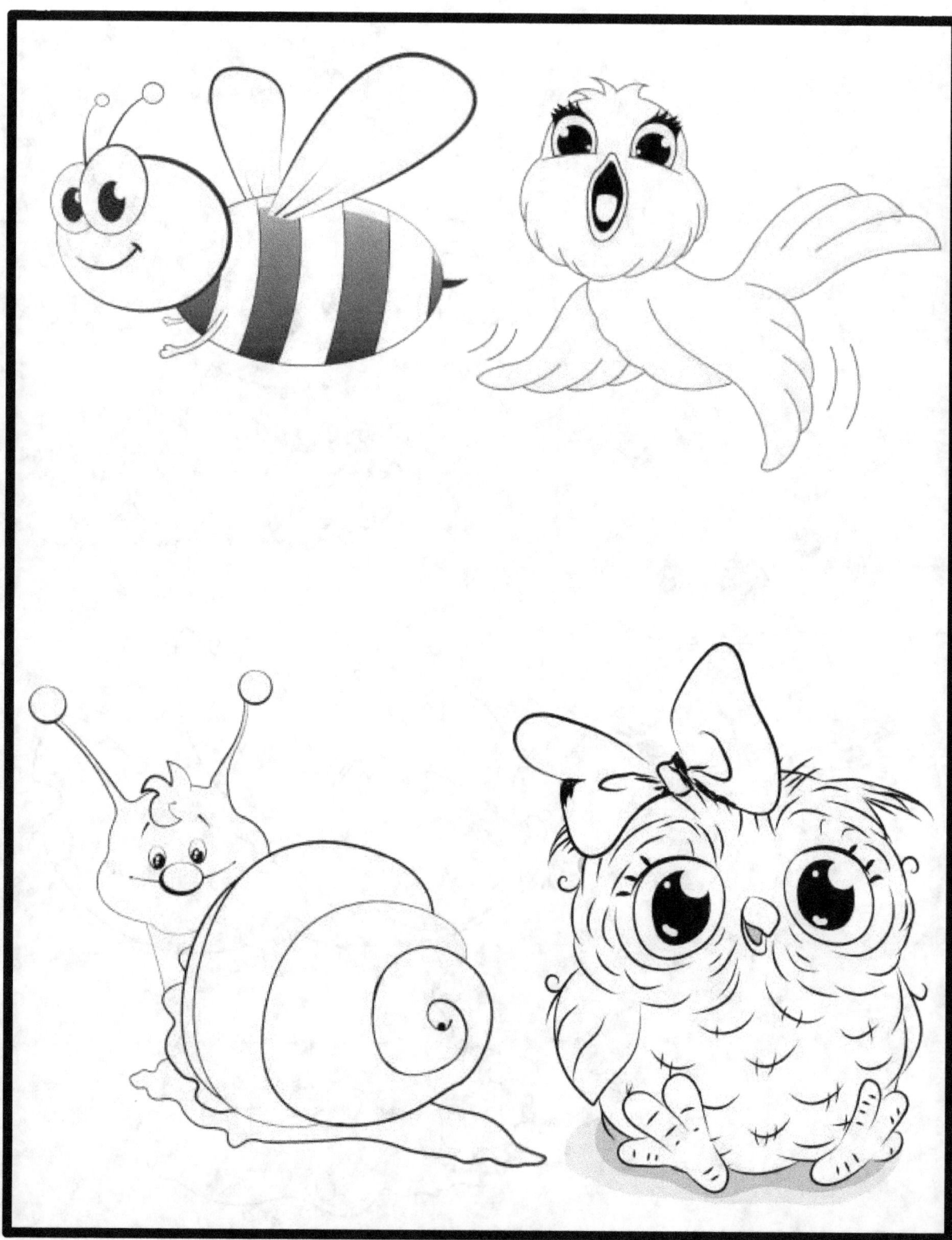

WHERE IS A BEAR ?

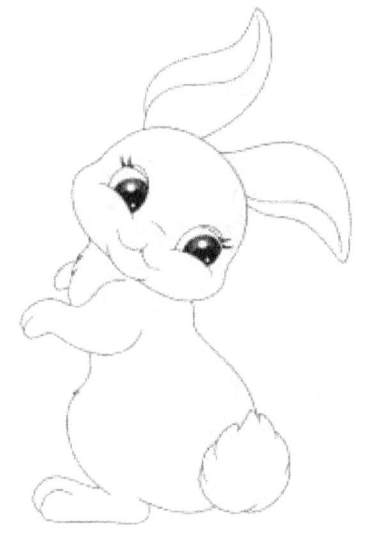
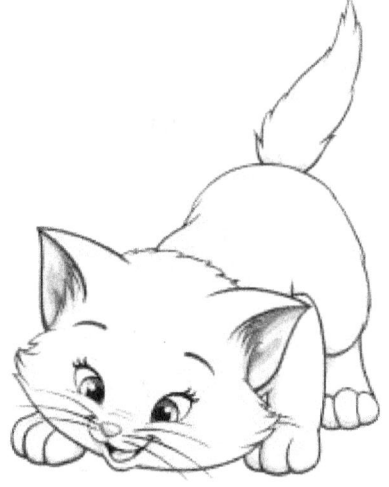
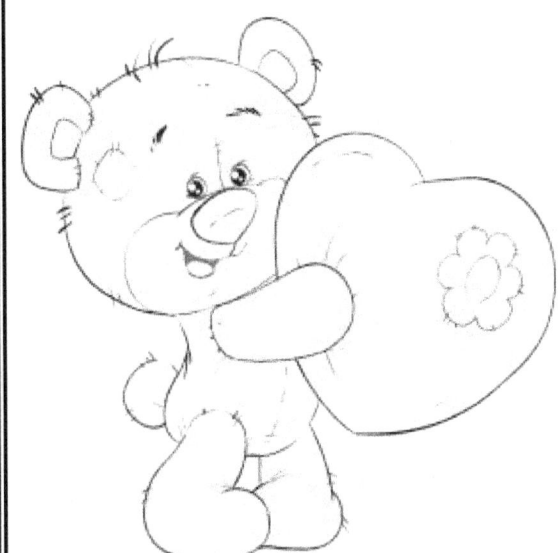
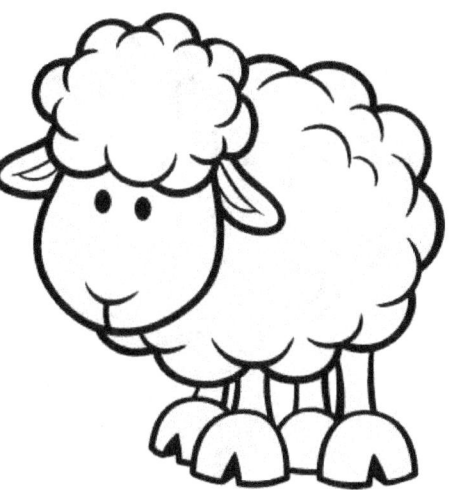

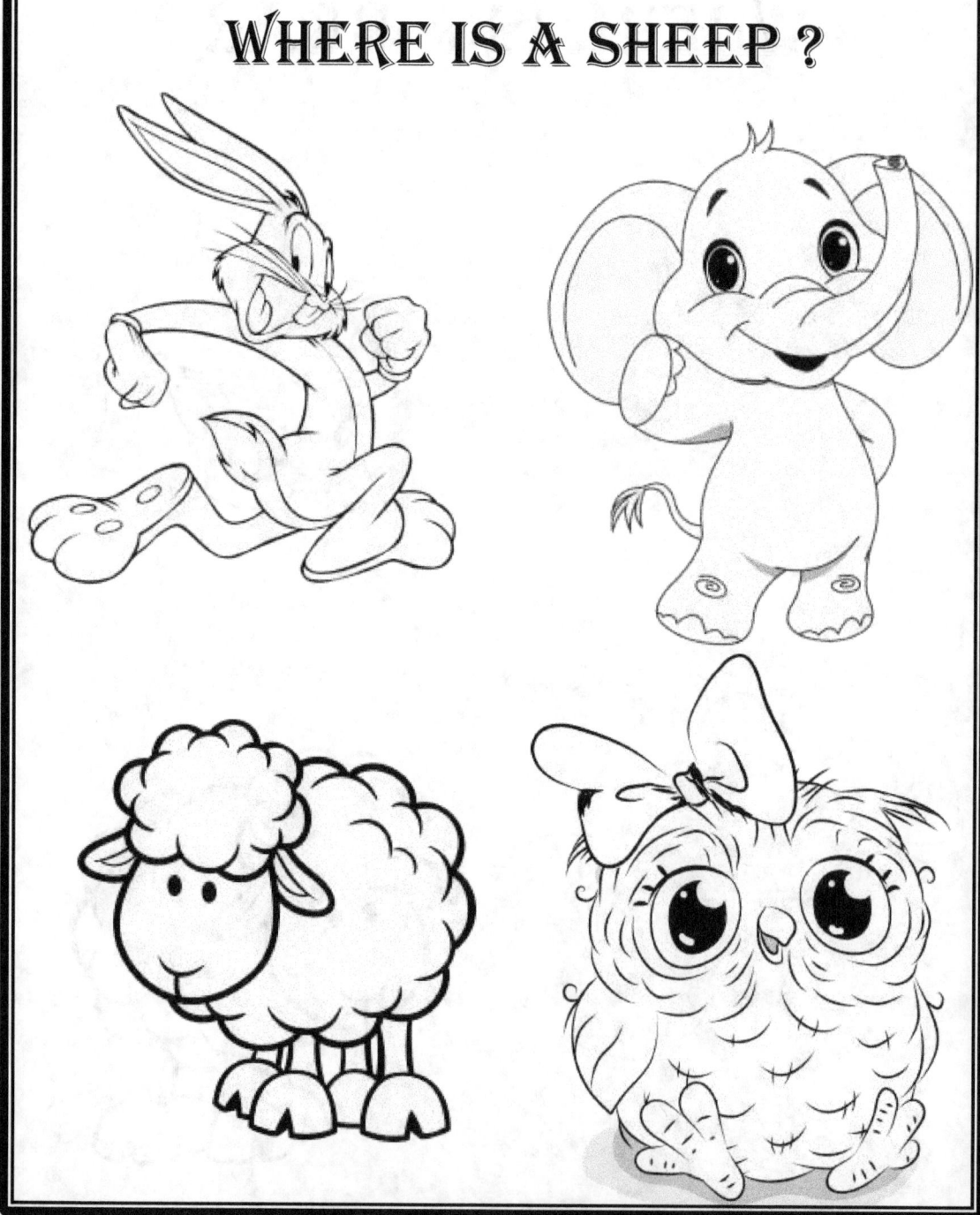

WHERE IS A COW?

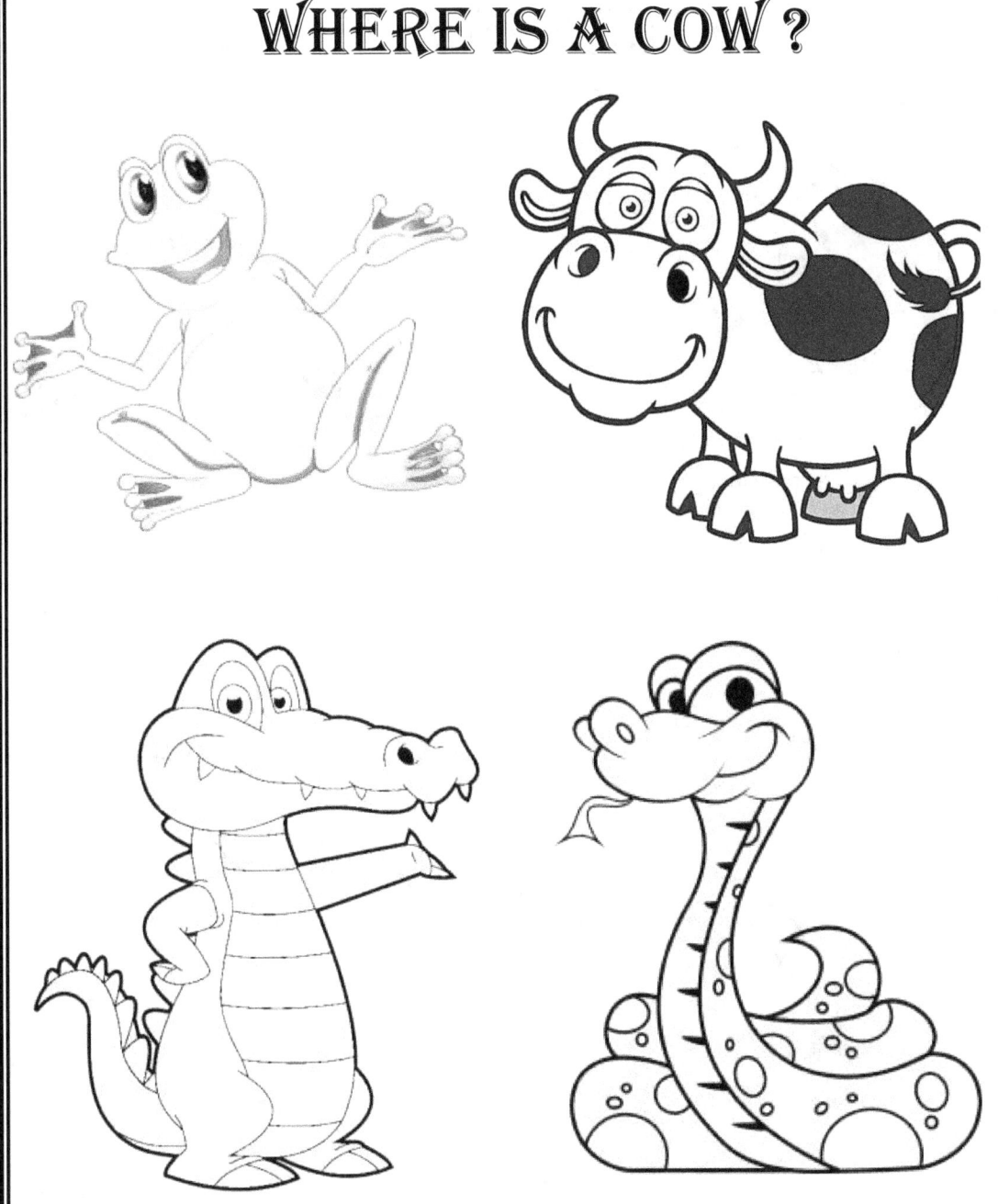

WHERE IS A FOX ?

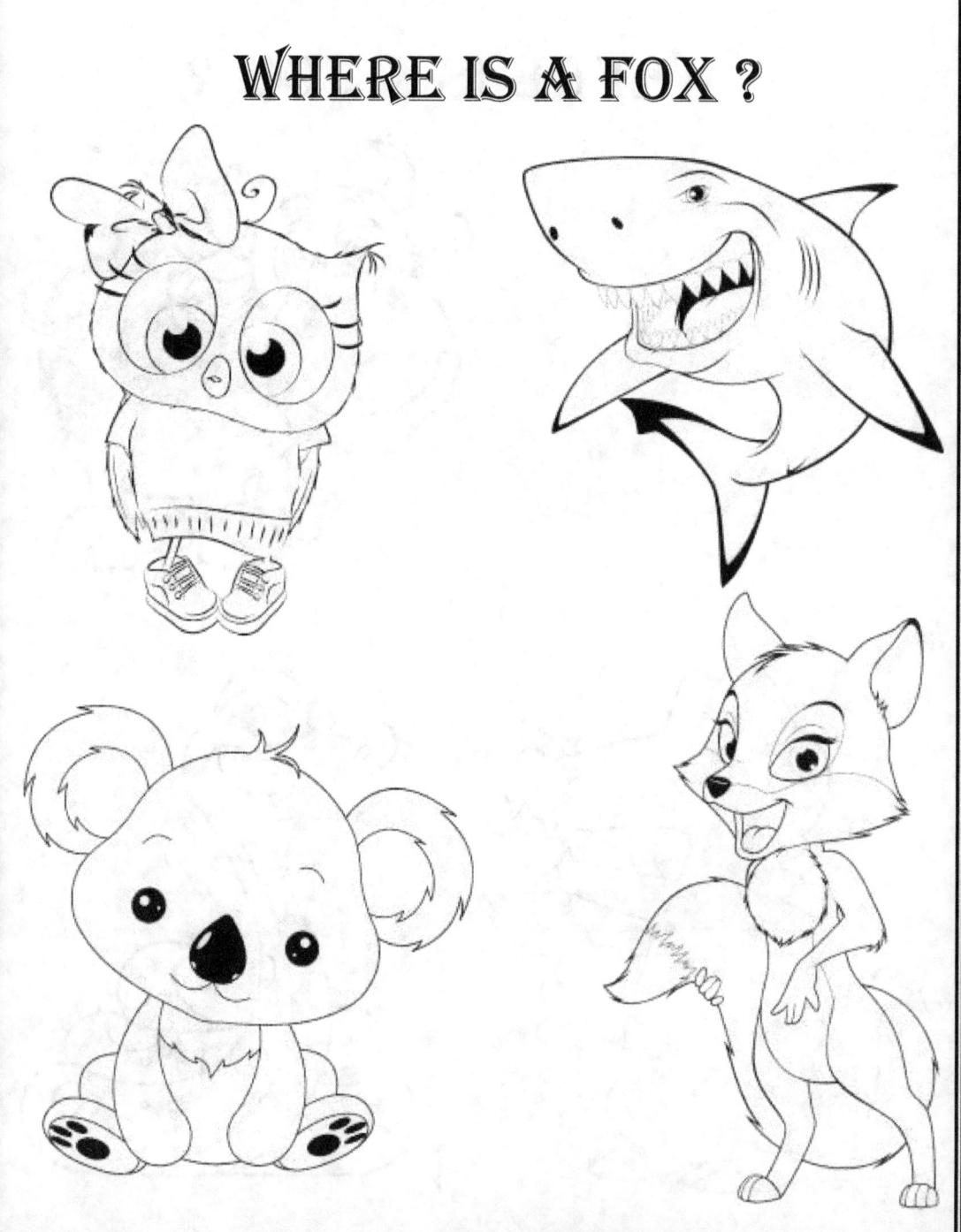

WHERE IS A KOALA ?

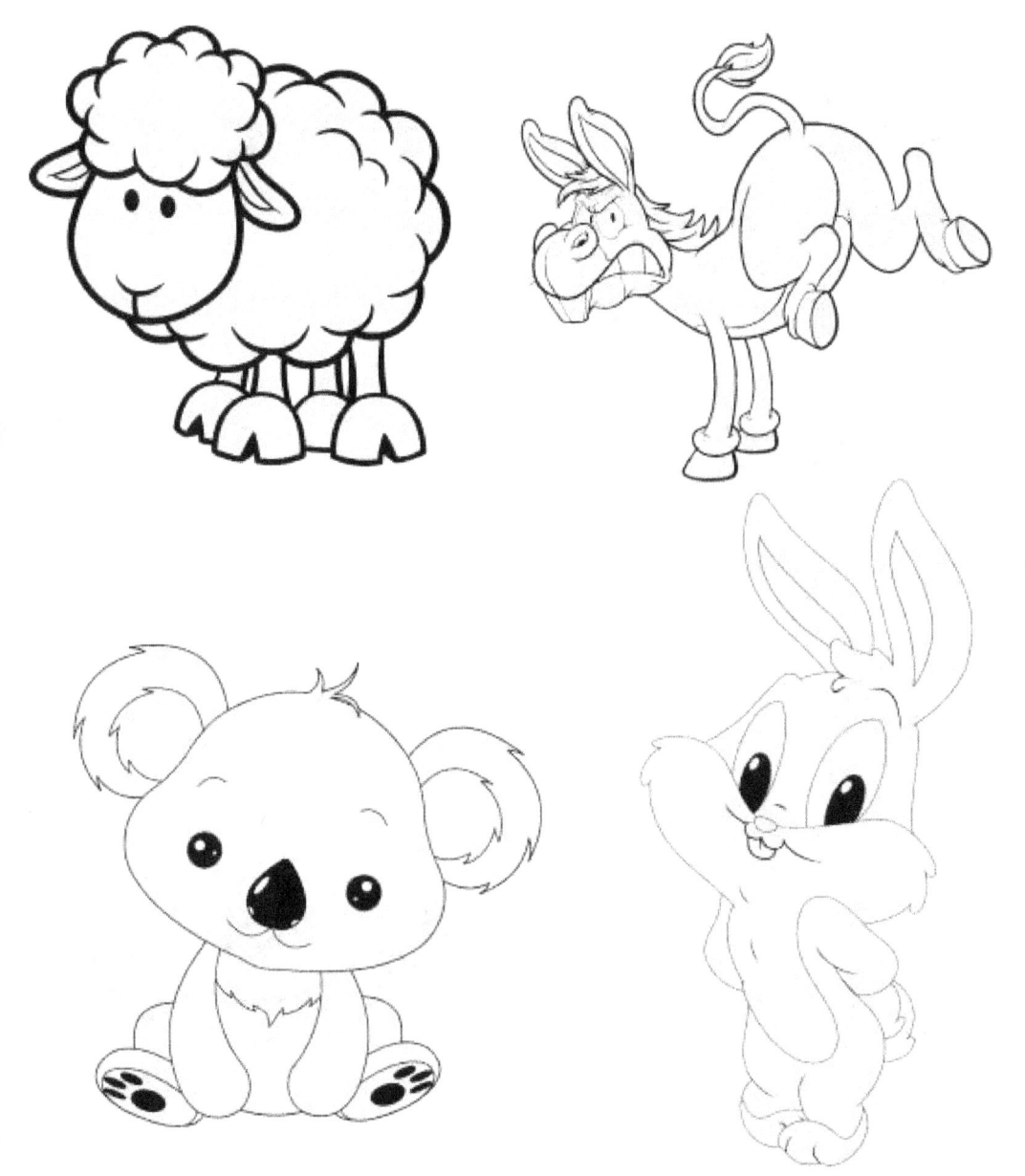

WHERE IS A LION?

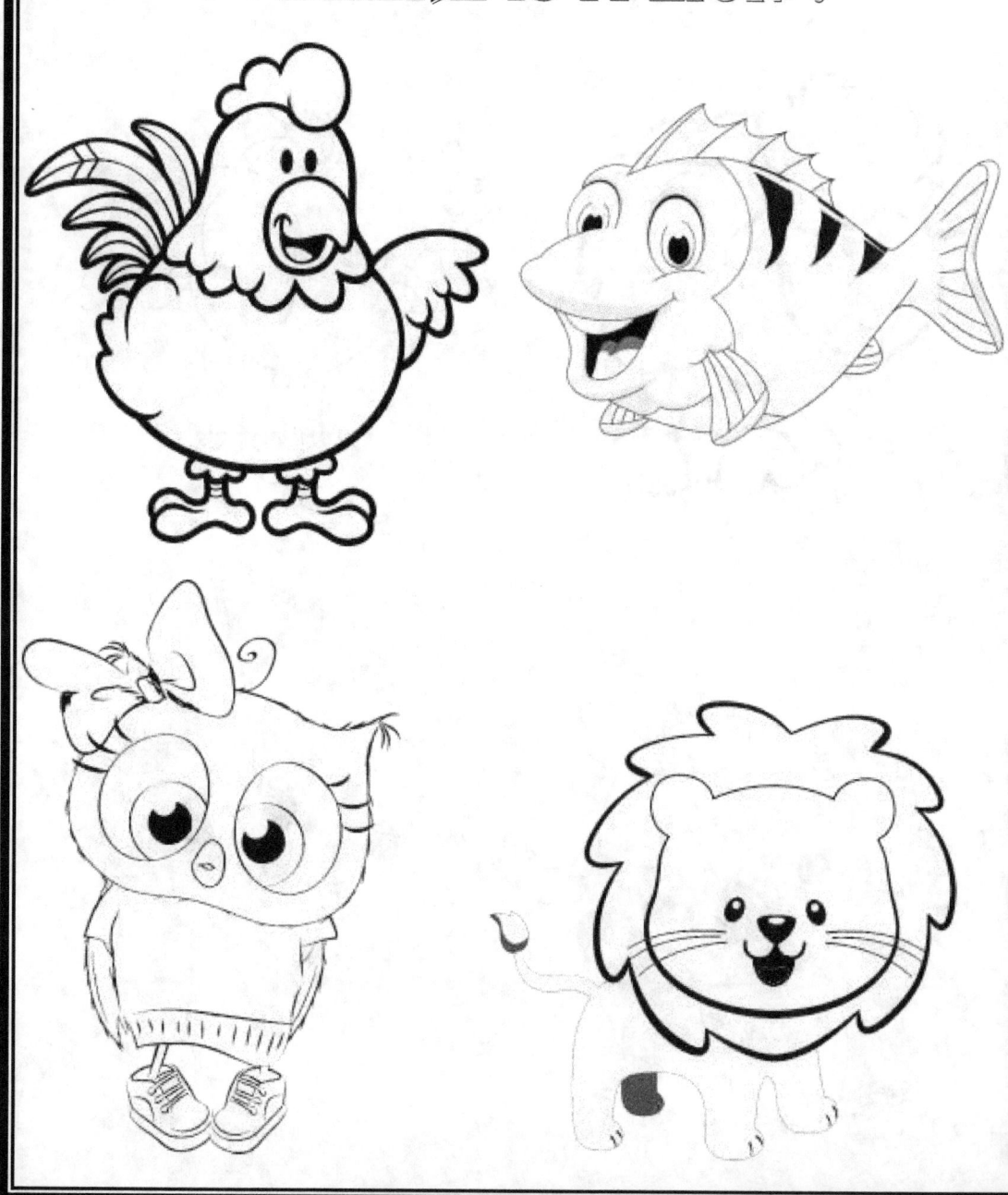

WHERE IS A COW?

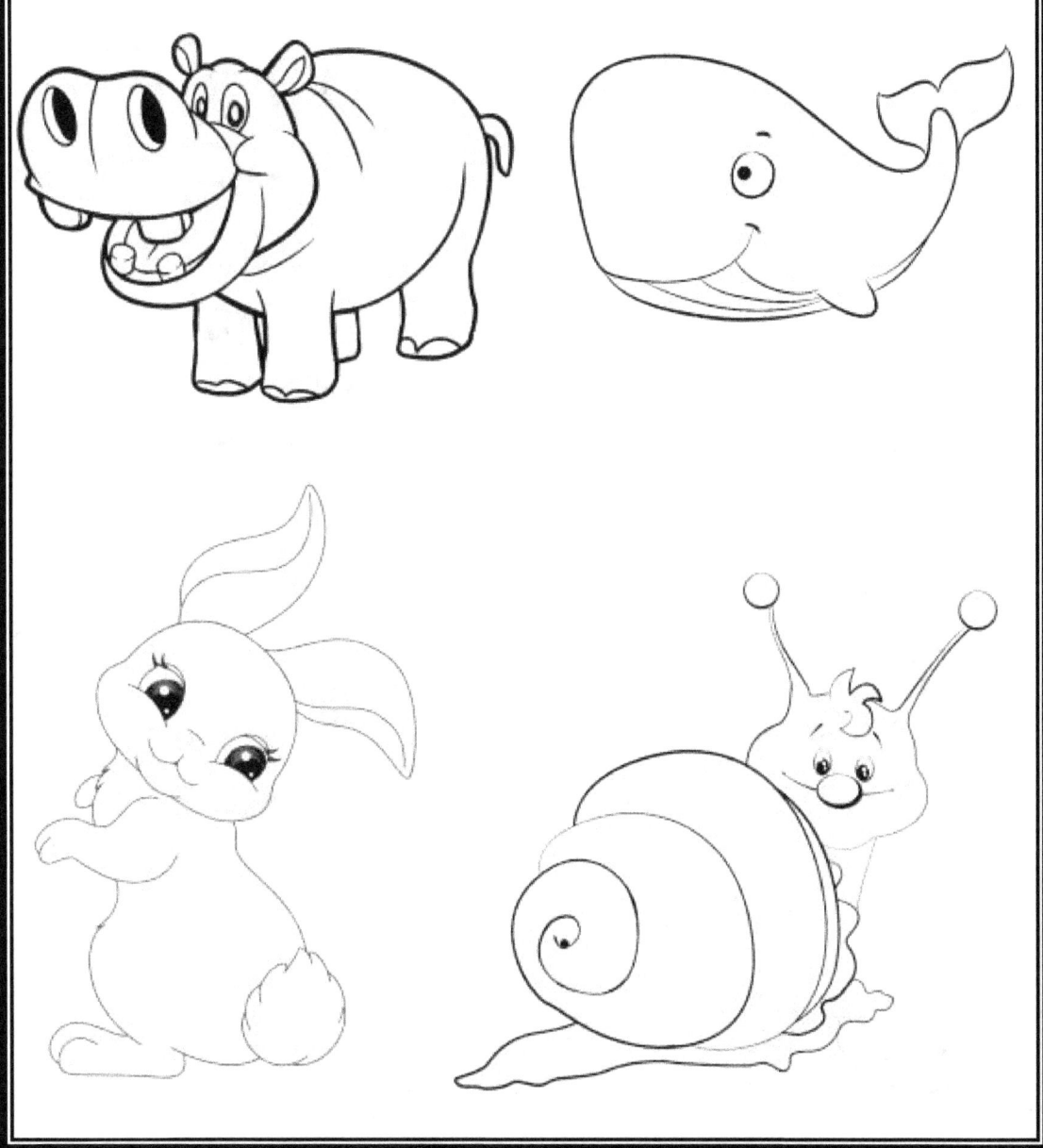

WHERE IS A MONKEY ?

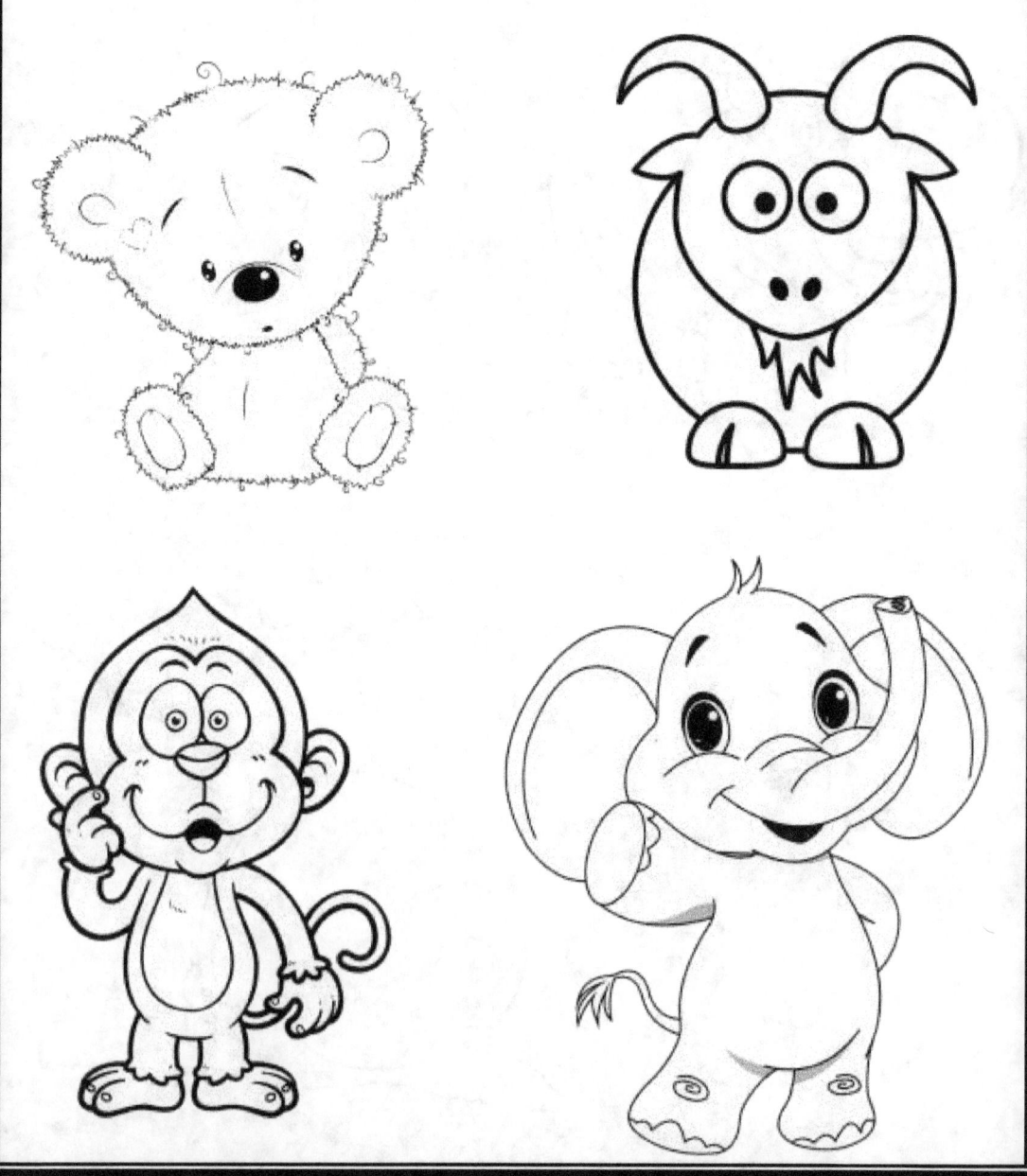

WHERE IS AN ELEPHANT?

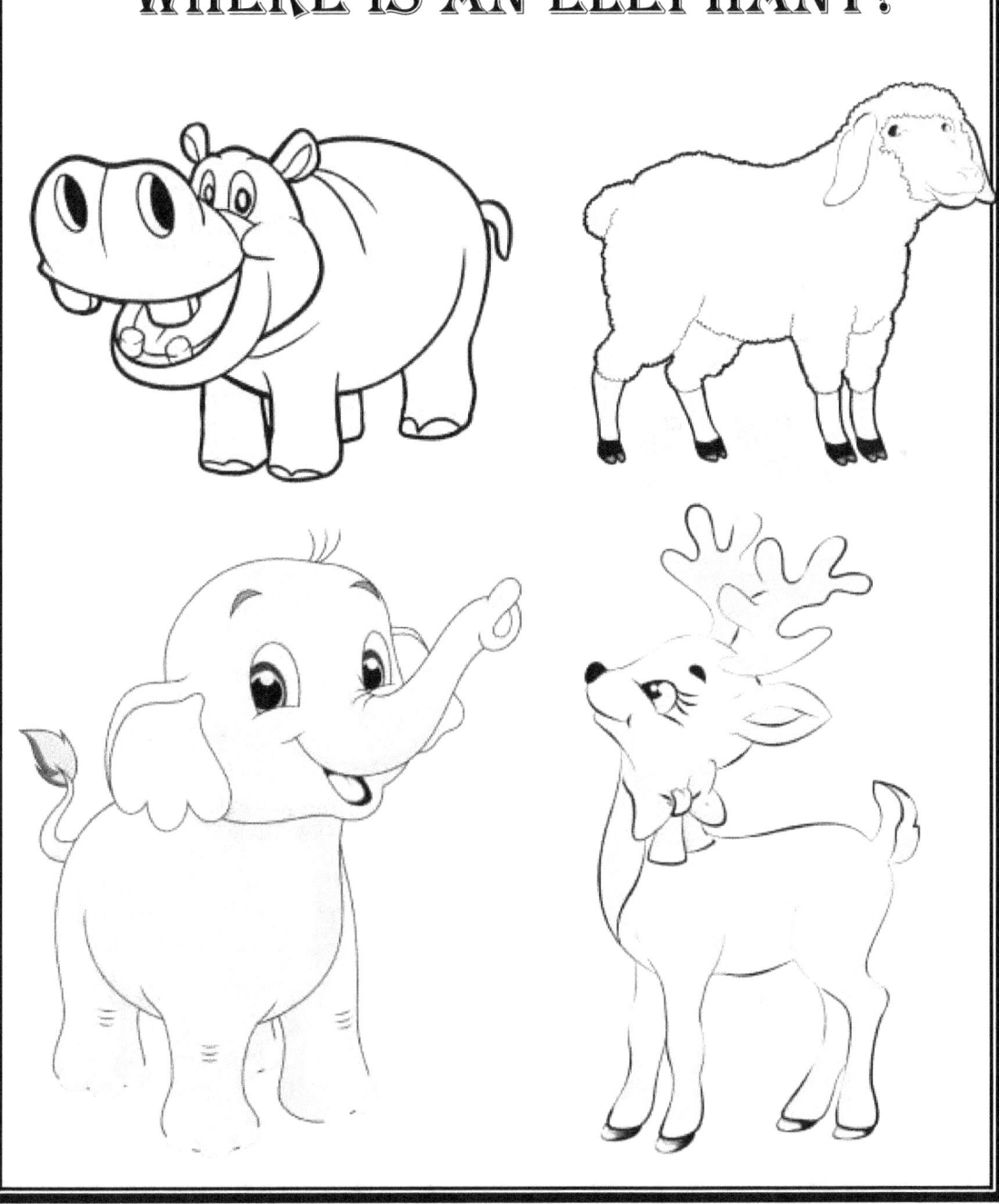

WHERE IS A RABBIT?

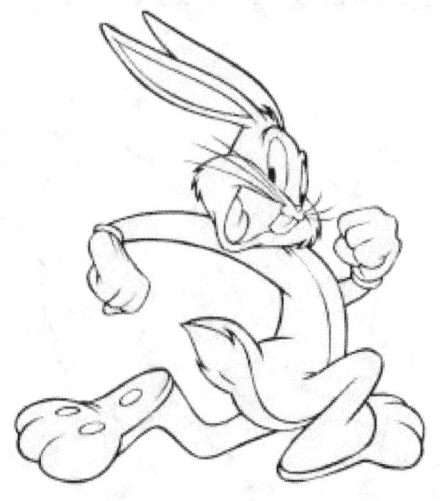
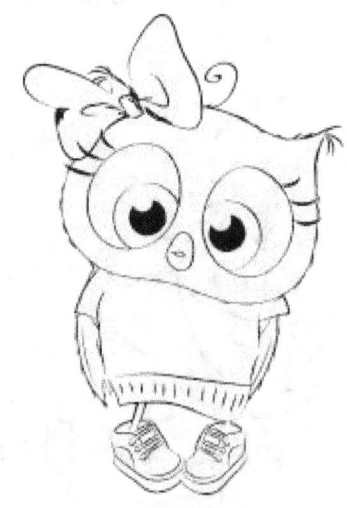
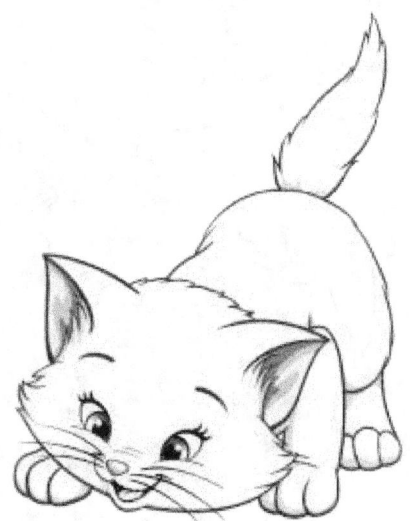
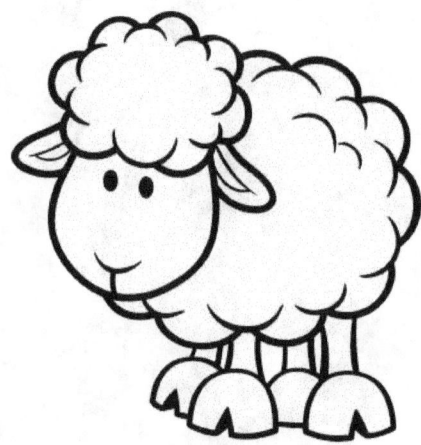